THE BANK EXECUTIVE'S GUIDE TO ENTERPRISE RISK MANAGEMENT

THE BANK EXECUTIVE'S GUIDE TO ENTERPRISE RISK MANAGEMENT

Contributing Editors
Robert Oberg
Tara Heusé Skinner

Contributors
Anat Bird
Ali Samad-Khan
Ladd Muzzy
Granger Souder
Maria Tabrizi
Karen Van de Castle
Ruth Yang

This publication is designed to provide accurate and authoritative information in regard to the subject matter covered. It is sold with the understanding that the publisher is not engaged in rendering legal, accounting, or other professional service. If legal advice or other expert assistance is required, the services of a competent professional person should be sought.

From a Declaration of Principles jointly adopted by a Committee of the American Bar Association and a Committee of Publishers and Associations.

The American Bankers Association is committed to providing innovative, high-quality products and services that are responsive to its members' critical needs.

To comment about this product, or to learn more about the American Bankers Association and the many products and services it offers, please call 1-800-BANKERS or visit our Web site: www.aba.com.

© Copyright 2006 by the American Bankers Association, Washington, D.C.

All rights reserved. No part of this publication may be reproduced, stored in a retrieval system, or transmitted in any form or by any means—electronic, mechanical, photocopying, recording, or otherwise—without prior written permission from the American Bankers Association.

10 9 8 7 6 5 4 3 2

Printed in the United States of America

PREFACE

Although enterprise risk management (ERM) is increasingly a critical function within banking, no standard structure or definition thoroughly explains it. In part, this is because ERM practices continue to evolve rapidly in response to varying levels of competition, management acumen, and regulatory pressures. As a result, ERM tends to mean different things to different people. Ask risk managers and bank executives to explain ERM, and you will get a variety of opinions. To those in bank compliance, ERM focuses on complying with the Bank Secrecy Act, Regulation O, and a host of other regulations; to bank auditors, ERM and the tenets of the Sarbanes-Oxley Act (SOX) are nearly synonymous and focus largely on internal controls.

In an effort to define ERM, the Council of Sponsoring Organizations of the Treadway Commission (COSO), a private sector organization made up principally of auditors and accountants, developed a blueprint of these professionals' recommendations for tackling ERM. Other audit industry professionals suggest that a bank's internal auditor not only should assess but, in some cases, should also oversee the risk management function. Some agencies, however, differ with this approach. For example, the Federal Reserve's latest bank holding company rating system assesses risk management within the context of board and management oversight, risk monitoring, internal controls, and policies, procedures, and limits. Academics and consultants define it as a comprehensive way to tackle the integration of all of the systems and people in an organization in managing uncertainties. The New Basel Capital Accord, or Basel II, which has taken a principal place in bank risk management, coordinates managing risks in the banking industry with risk-measurement models to calculate the amount of capital to be set aside for unexpected losses from an investor's and a bank regulator's perspective.

One thing is certain: ERM is not a fad. It is a strategic business decision and a subject that all banks have to address. And while traditional views of risk management focus on audit and compliance practices, ERM is, in fact, much more.

What we did *not* discover in our efforts to implement ERM in our respective organizations (a definition of ERM exclusively from a banker's perspective) prompted us to compile this guide. *The Bank Executive's Guide to Enterprise Risk Management* is a call to the banking industry to define ERM for itself, borrowing, if you will, from the best the auditors, consultants, insurance industry, and regulators have to offer, but making ERM uniquely its own.

Bank regulatory agencies are focusing on processes banks are implementing to identify, assess, monitor, and manage risks. Enterprise risk management has become the standard to which banks are building their risk management programs. Generally, enterprise risk management means integrating all risks through a central risk management process with a chief risk manager at the helm.

Although the depth and breadth of risk management programs vary, all bank managers and directors must remember some basic tenets to every process:

- Risk management is a process that will both add and protect shareholder value.
- Risk must be managed on an enterprise-wide basis.
- The best measure of risk versus reward is risk-adjusted return on capital.
- ERM must be independent.
- Risk management is not an audit function or a compliance function.

Despite regulatory pressure, bank managers and directors should not implement risk management processes merely to satisfy regulators. Instead, they should do so because it makes good business sense. Banking analysts and shareholders should demand effective risk management programs that exceed the expectations of regulators. When implemented effectively, enterprise risk management will transcend COSO's traditional audit and control processes and shift resources from bank compliance and crisis management to strategic planning, capital management, and enhancing shareholder value.

      Robert Oberg   Tara Heusé Skinner
      Cincinnati, Ohio   Greenville, South Carolina

ABOUT *THE BANK EXECUTIVE'S GUIDE TO ENTERPRISE RISK MANAGEMENT*

There are many business reasons to adopt more sophisticated methods to measure and manage financial services risks, not just regulatory ones. All of the models constructed to date employ stringent statistical measurement and a team of mathematicians, neither of which makes sense for the smaller regional or community bank. This book is for them: the smaller regional and community banks that seek to manage risk without literally breaking the bank.

    This book discusses both the "art and science" behind enterprise risk management. It will give smaller banks cost-effective tools with which they can successfully measure their risks and thereby benefit from better pricing and better risk-to-capital management.

    Even though it is a compilation, this book has a clear and simple unifying theme: manage the risks in the bank and rewards follow. The contributing authors are all practitioners in the financial services industry, and none of them is content to allow the industry to define enterprise risk management for them. Instead, the contributors have painstakingly defined it, and continue to define it, for themselves. This book is the product of the definitions they want to share with you, the bank executive.

ORGANIZATION OF THE BOOK

The Bank Executive's Guide to Enterprise Risk Management is divided into three parts. Part 1, "The Business Case for ERM," describes solid business reasons for adopting ERM best practices and presenting ERM adoption to executive management and the bank's board of directors. Chapter 1 is central to those goals—encouraging the bank executive to explore available options and thereby help develop strategies that increase earnings and manage capital. Chapter 2 dispels the argument against adopting more sophisticated practices to measure, model, and manage risks; it argues instead that these tasks are done best within the context of one's own banking and company traditions. This is a key chapter. It will help a bank executive to overcome cultural roadblocks inherent in a bank's organization. Chapter 3 provides a suggested framework bank executives can use to organize infrastructure for supporting ERM. It explains the role internal audit plays in ERM and how each complements the other.

Part 2, "Understanding Banking Risks," explores three broad categories of bank risks: credit, market, and operational. Credit risk, covered in chapter 4, explores fundamental concepts used to measure risk in a credit portfolio, beyond traditional underwriting methods. Chapter 5, Market Risk, covers interest rate risk and liquidity risk—the two most significant market risks that affect the community banker. It also discusses an important risk measure: Value-at-Risk (VAR). Chapter 6, Operational Risk, explores many subcategories of operational risks. Chapter 6 is most diverse in thought and application.

Part 3, "Integrating ERM into the Organization," offers measures the practitioner can use when measuring risk. Together with the discussion of VAR in chapter 5, Part 3 is as heady as the *Guide* gets. ERM for larger banks is expensive because they have to adopt complicated systems to measure and model their risks. Not only do they have to purchase or build complete technology systems, but also they have to hire statisticians and economists. Chapter 7 spells out simple methods for measuring risks. Although not Basel II compliant by any means, chapter 7 gives the bank executive some basic methodology that expands on the risks inherent in bank portfolios and in a bank's practices. Chapter 8 details the concept of economic capital, an important measure of risk, and the fundamental component in measuring the risks embedded in portfolios, products, and lines of business.

The appendices provide samples for creating a bank's risk management plan, policy, and procedures. They also list the elements of an ERM committee charter and include job descriptions of a chief risk officer and other risk management professionals. They contain, as well, a sample risk profile report the bank executive can use to effectively report the status of risk in the bank.

ACKNOWLEDGMENTS

This book is based on research originally presented at various banking conferences and seminars. Over the years, I have consulted with many directors, senior managers, federal regulators, and other risk scholars and practitioners in an effort to refine my views on the practical implementation of an effective risk management program. I wish to thank Bill Wells for his patience as a mentor and the latitude given me to try new ideas. In addition, I wish to thank Jim Gerti and other chief risk officers with whom I have worked and whose teachings have contributed so much to my understanding of enterprise risk management. I especially thank those colleagues and friends, particularly at the Federal Reserve and Comptroller of the Currency, who continue to encourage me to find ways to transform conceptual aspects of risk management into a practical application of risk management. Finally, I am grateful to the many people who have worked with me to execute the company's risk management program. I truly recognize that they are the muscle that makes enterprise risk management effective. Without their significant contributions, my knowledge of enterprise risk management would remain purely theoretical. No doubt some of these colleagues will disagree with some aspects of my conclusions, for which I take full responsibility.

I extend a heartfelt note of appreciation to all of the authors who contributed their time and shared their knowledge so that this book may be a success.

R.C.O.

From its inception, this book was meant to be a compilation of ideas from bankers. But the contributors to the content of *The Bank Executive's Guide to Enterprise Risk Management* do not stop with those listed as authors of the text. The contents herein benefited greatly from the comments by skilled risk professionals, academics, and practitioners alike. Any errors that linger belong to the editors.

I wish to thank Paul Skinner, Sandra Halperin, and Iris Saltiel for sharing their skill, ideas, encouragement, and inspiration. Most especially, I would like to express deep gratitude to my co-editor, Robert Oberg, for his hard work, the idea of putting this book together, and his selfless partnership in this endeavor.

T.H.S.

Preface

The American Bankers Association also wants to thank the following bankers for their careful reviews and thoughtful comments on this book:

Nicki Brown	President & CEO The Wilton Bank Wilton, Connecticut
Kathleen Bruegenhemke	Senior Vice President Exchange National Bancshares, Inc. Jefferson City, Missouri
Barbara Buss	Vice President TCF Bank Minneapolis, Minnesota
Walt Winter, Jr.	Chief Executive Officer and General Counsel Peoples Bank Lawrence, Kansas

TABLE OF CONTENTS

Part 1: The Business Case for ERM — 1

Chapter 1   ERM: a Strategic Decision   3
Tara Heusé Skinner

Chapter 2   ERM and the Bank's Culture   13
Tara Heusé Skinner and Anat Bird

Chapter 3   Creating the Proper Infrastructure to Maximize ERM   27
Robert Oberg and Maria Tabrizi

Part 2: Understanding Bank Risks — 53

Chapter 4   Credit Risk   55
Karen Van de Castle and Ruth Yang

Chapter 5   Market Risk   69
Tara Heusé Skinner

Chapter 6   Operational Risk   83
Ali Samad-Khan, Ladd Muzzy, Robert Oberg, Granger Souder, and Tara Heusé Skinner

Part 3: Integrating ERM into the Organization — 123

Chapter 7   Integrating Bank Risks Through Measurement   125
Tara Heusé Skinner

Chapter 8   Economic Capital and Decision Making   133
Robert Oberg and Tara Heusé Skinner

Appendices — 145

  A. ERM Job Descriptions — 147
  B. Risk Management Plan — 163
  C. Risk Management Policy — 165
  D. Risk Management Procedures — 173
  E. Elements of an Enterprise Risk Management Committee Charter — 177
  F. Enterprise Risk Management Organizational Chart — 179
  G. Sample Risk Profile Report for the Board of Directors — 181

Notes — 189
Glossary — 199
Bibliography — 203
About the Contributors — 211
Index — 215

PART 1
THE BUSINESS CASE FOR ERM

The bank executive performs the delicate dance of running a profitable business while complying with bank regulations without being held hostage by them. It is a tough waltz, particularly when there appears to be incongruence between the objectives of regulation and legislation and managing net income and capital, offering products and services, and creating shareholder value.

Enterprise risk management, if left to conventional wisdom or irrational exuberance, will quickly become another compliance exercise, the regulation *du jour*. The first part of this guide covers why adopting ERM practices is simply good business for banks and, if done within the context of the bank's culture and today's post-9/11 and post-Enron environment, can mean significant increases in earnings, no matter what the size of the organization.

Chapter 1
ERM: A Strategic Decision

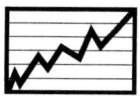

Qui ne risqué rien n'a rien
(nothing ventured, nothing gained)
French proverb

The word "risk" originates in the Latin *risicum*, the word for a barrier reef.[1] To sailors, a barrier reef means both the challenge of getting past it unscathed and moving toward the opportunities beyond. Sadly, the modern day English meaning takes on the negative connotation alone. Risk management has come to mean the avoidance or mitigation of things that ail us. It does not include the promise of a positive outcome.

Formula for Success

A bank executive who views enterprise risk management (ERM) simply as a compliance exercise loses much in winning in the marketplace. Success will come if the bank executive:

- views enterprise risk management as a competitive business strategy
- finds the economic incentives that ERM has for the banking organization

---

This chapter promotes an understanding of what ERM is and what it is not. It also offers strategies for the bank executive to capitalize on the competitive advantages ERM provides.

UNDERSTANDING ENTERPRISE RISK MANAGEMENT

Enterprise risk management (ERM) is the consolidated, more structured management of uncertainties that either positively or negatively influence the activities of a bank as it seeks to create value,[2] *not* just those uncertainties that negatively influence activities.

The executive looking to ERM as the silver bullet to cure the company's woes about regulatory and SOX compliance misses the point of managing risks for the bank on an enterprise level. In fact, the executive is leaving quite of bit of money on the table. Valuable and tangible economic incentives exist for viewing the various risks *and* the opportunities that come with them. In short, ERM makes good business sense.

In managing enterprise risk, there are two distinct incentives for increasing a company's level of sophistication: (1) avoiding the enormous price that the mismanagement of risk can carry, and (2) increasing the company's income.

The "Traditional" Definition of ERM

The traditional view of enterprise risk management comes primarily from an insurance perspective. That is, is the bank covered in the case of calamity? Risk management focuses on the personal safety of customers and employees and the restoration of physical assets if disaster strikes.

Expand the definition of ERM as it relates to banks and financial services, and the term gets broader. A loan officer underwrites a loan in accordance with the borrower's ability to repay *and* the collateral behind the loan. Both issues play a part in the risk decision behind the credit.

Capital requirements for banks broadened the definition to include Value-at-Risk (VAR) models, so that banks could set their capital requirements to compensate for market risk. The Sarbanes-Oxley Act expanded the known definitions to include internal controls over financial reporting.

To boards of directors, risk management now includes being aware of the penalties of the U.S. Sentencing Guidelines and ensuring that a program of corporate compliance and business ethics is in place and working in the organization.

In short, ask for the definition of ERM and one will probably get as many answers as there are people asked. The overall definition is that ERM includes all of those definitions, but it also should encompass this concept: *ERM is a business strategy with clear, material economic benefits to a bank that practices a more advanced level of risk measurement and management than advocated by more traditional approaches.*

ERM Evolution

Do the risks of one business line affect another? In a word, yes! For the most part, however, risks are managed throughout an organization in what have come to be known as silos, or lines of business. Each line manager is expected to manage, mitigate, and control the risks that his or her line pose to the bank's business. ERM, however, takes risk management one step further. It considers the risks of the entire organization, across business lines, to see how those risks relate to and affect one another.[3]

For the most part, with Basel II provisions and the Federal Reserve's 2005 Bank Holding Company Rating System, ERM is now more of a framework for integrating all areas of risk management into a consolidated view for the executive level. It is indeed a business strategy, and when incorporated effectively within an organization, it can aid tremendously in management's business decisions.

Regulation, however, is not the driver for ERM. Though it may seem that ERM is the tail wagging the dog, effective business practices, in fact, have enlightened an industry shouldering increased regulation. Pioneering banks developed the tools to both measure the risk of a transaction and to be properly compensated for that risk. The banking industry has adopted many sophisticated models already, but smaller banks have not always capitalized on the financial rewards they offer, particularly in better managing credit risks and in mitigating operational risks.

To Basel or Not to Basel: Size Doesn't Matter

In 1988, the Basel committee of the Bank for International Settlements published the Basel Capital Accord, which provides procedures for capital held for credit risk. It applied only to those banks that operated internationally. At that time, capital set aside for the risks that the banking industry was taking was considered inadequate. This first Basel Accord (known as "Basel") was quickly adopted as the global standard. Its provisions went well beyond internationally operating banks, even though it treated all markets and portfolios in the same way. Regardless of size or business model, banks had to (and still do) set aside a minimum of 8 percent of their risk-adjusted assets in capital, despite the level of risk inherent in their books of business.

In the mid-1990s, Basel was expanded to include market risk. Soon afterward, the Basel committee began to draft the New Basel Capital Accord (or "Basel II"), which includes provisions for measuring operational risk. Basel II's principles stress that capital allocations should be closely aligned with the actual risks a bank holds determined by its own practices and portfolios, not with some predetermined "one-size-fits-all" estimate.

In the United States, capital standards are higher than those of the first Basel Accord; consequently, Basel is barely noticed domestically. In Europe and Asia, however, the announcement of Basel II sent many banks scurrying to get their economic and regulatory capital houses in order. Until recently, Basel II in the United States went largely unnoticed, and the vast majority of smaller banks ignored it.

This is unfortunate for two reasons. First, when William J. McDonough, former president and CEO of the Federal Reserve

Board of New York, was chairman of the Basel committee, he gave all banks a clear motivation to stay the course. He stated that the Basel committee "expressly designed the New Accord *to provide tangible economic incentives for banks to adopt increasingly sophisticated risk management practices.*"[4] (italics ours). By measuring risk levels in a loan portfolio, the risk decision is placed in the hands of the relationship manager. The bank is properly compensated for the risks taken, and asset quality improves. Additionally, more sophisticated methodology can improve a banker's ability to identify and mitigate risks inherent in the banking operation.

Second, the banks adopting Basel II, though few in number, represent over 75 percent of all U.S. banking assets. In the United States, 60 percent of all commercial loans have the most advanced internal ratings-based measures available.[5] Like it or not, non-Basel II banks are competing head-to-head with banks that are required to comply with Basel II and can, among other things (see below), lower pricing to all of the best customers in their markets.

MAKING THE CASE FOR ERM

Basel II is here to stay, and it has far-reaching implications for non-Basel II banks.[6] Arguably, compliance with the most advanced internal ratings-based models is too costly for smaller banks that can never hope to benefit from the economic incentives built into the new Basel Accord. To an extent, this is true. Almost 40 percent of U.S. and Canadian banks that must comply with Basel II expect costs to reach $30 million; 20 percent estimate that it will cost significantly more than that.[7]

U.S. federal banking agencies (Federal Reserve, FDIC, OCC, and OTS) determined that the advanced-risk methodology (which is behind Basel II) applies only to the ten-to-twenty largest banking firms in the country. Although the standards will not apply to smaller banks, it appears that for the large banking firms that adopt them, the new standards will lead to significant competitive advantages in:

- lower capital requirements
- reduced operational losses
- better pricing decisions
- improved asset quality

Consequently, the remaining 7,800 plus U.S. banks will have to maintain a competitive balance within the industry.

This is where smaller banks have an advantage over larger banks. Smaller banks can adopt simpler (and cheaper) approaches to ERM and can do so within their own time frames (think of it as "Basel lite"). In so doing, adopting banks can gain economic and competitive advantages as well as regulatory compliance.

Economic Incentives

Research indicates that by adopting more complex models to measure and manage risks, bank management can improve its pretax earnings by 3 to 6 percent.[8] Most banks, by using traditional pricing methods, are not properly compensated for the risks they take when lending money to their customers. By properly pricing loans to the risk they carry, banks can increase their profit margins.

In client work performed by McKinsey & Company, four risk management efficiencies are identified along with their expected pretax earnings increases (see exhibit 1.1).

Most of the economic benefits come from better identification, measurement, and management of credit risks. By developing better credit risk management methodologies (see chapter 4 for an indepth explanation), banks should experience better default prediction and improved collection processes and pricing discipline. Lowering operating expenses by improving operations, such as streamlining underwriting processes, also benefits banks.

Exhibit 1.1 Risk Management Efficiencies

Improvement Effort	Increase to Pretax Earnings
1. Reduced charge-offs	1%
2. Risk-based pricing	1% to 2%
3. Streamlined underwriting processes	0.5% to 1%
4. Operational loss mitigation	1% to 2%
Overall improvement	3.5% to 6%

Source: McKinsey & Company, 2005.

Developing additional ways to identify and measure operational risks (those risks not attributed to the credit portfolio or to the market) enables a bank to gain two other economic advantages: (1) it can better predict and possibly avoid future losses and retain capital, and (2) it can mitigate current losses. When a bank begins to view new business opportunities with an eye for risk management, the overall risk profile of products, services, and activities, such as acquisitions and *de novos*, is lowered. Chapter 6 provides methods to identify and measure operational risks in order to maximize the benefits of improved operational risk management.

THE GREAT DIVIDE

Even if non-Basel II banks continue to ignore the advanced-risk models, outside parties will not. The more sophisticated practices of ERM have caused a divide within the U.S. banking industry. The ten to twenty largest banks in the country have no choice; they must adopt more sophisticated methodology designed for capital allocation (see exhibit 1.2 for a comparison of traditional and advanced methodology). With the Federal Reserve Bank's 2005 ratings system, larger, complex bank holding companies also are being nudged in that direction.

EXHIBIT 1.2 Traditional versus Advanced Risk Models Pricing

	Traditional Banks	Advanced (Risk-Based Models) Banks
Pricing	Traditional, linear pricing	Risk-based pricing
Capital Allocation for Credit Risks	Flat 8 percent capital charge	Matching economic capital allocations to actual risks
Operational Risks	Current level of loss	Mitigated losses, lower capital allocations

On the one hand are banks that practice highly developed ways to identify, measure, model, and manage their risk. On the other hand are banks that choose not to adopt basic methodology to measure risk effectively. Given the two different scenarios, consider the view from insurance underwriters, Wall Street, and ratings agencies such as Moody's and Standard & Poor's.

- *Corporate insurance companies.* Premiums and coverage directly correspond to the insurance companies' view of a bank's risk profile. Healthier risk management translates into lower premiums and higher coverage.
- *Wall Street.* For publicly traded banks, the viewpoints of investment analysts are quite important. Given a choice to recommend a bank's stock for purchase, will they select by performance only, or will they include their perception of the strength of the bank's management and its practices? Investment analyst's choices directly influence the market capitalization of a bank.
- *Ratings agencies* view publicly traded banks according to how well they manage their risks. If opportunities to increase pretax earnings, as outlined above, hold no appeal for the smaller bank, perhaps the costs and availability of funds will. More advanced ways of managing risks may not bolster a bank's rating, but at the very least, they will give agencies a good reason to hold to the current rating. Conversely, not adopting a superior methodology may affect the rating negatively. When analyzing

the business case for advanced ERM techniques, management may be surprised to learn how much an agency rating downgrade may affect its cost of funds.

COUNTING THE COSTS

Will these benefits outweigh the seemingly insurmountable costs involved in initiating ERM practices within smaller banks? As mentioned, smaller banks have two advantages their larger counterparts do not: they can adopt simpler, less expensive methodologies, and they can do it within their own time frame.

It is important to remember that there is no ideal solution to bringing a bank up to par using more sophisticated means to measure risks. Models can be built inhouse or purchased, and the price associated with each type differs greatly, not only from vendor to vendor but from bank to bank. The costs also will vary with the time a bank takes to adopt the models for measuring credit, market, and operational risks. Inexpensive models can be built inhouse by following the guidelines presented later in this book (Parts 2 and 3) and can be performed on a project-by-project basis within the time constraints set by bank management. Regardless of method and time frame, however, it is clear that significant costs are associated with *not* adopting ERM.

Key Points

ERM: a Strategic Decision

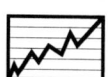

- ► Adopting advanced methodologies for identifying, measuring, modeling, and managing risks can result in a 3 to 6 percent increase in pretax earnings.
- ► Smaller banks have an advantage over larger competitors; they can adopt simpler and cheaper ERM methodologies and work within their own schedules while still gaining the economic advantages promised by ERM.

Chapter 2
ERM AND THE BANK'S CULTURE

Ambition has no risk.
Edward George Earle Bulwer-Lytton (1803–1873),
playwright, *Richelieu*, Act iii. Sc. i.

There's a legend at Federal Express that tells of a driver who, when getting to the last drop box of the day, realized that he had no key with which to open it. Since he did not have the time to drive back to his home base to get the key and return to the drop box, ensuring that the box's contents would get to their destinations as FedEx promises, he made a quick decision. He ripped the box out of the ground, taking the box to the key rather than bringing the key to the box.

At FedEx, he's considered a hero. His counterpart at the U.S. Postal Service, if he did the same thing, however, probably would be considered a thief. FedEx and the U.S.P.S.—two companies with very similar business models, but two very different cultures.

Formula for Success

There is no secret to successfully implementing an ERM in a bank. Just remember to:

- ► Match the implementation strategy to the bank's culture.
- ► Consider the individual values of the most successful people in the organization.
- ► Work within the culture given you; do not try to change the culture.

This chapter provides bank executives with strategies for implemening ERM within the context of their bank's culture. It will help bankers determine the culture of the organization and give practical applications for matching the strategy for implementation with the collective values of the people in the bank.

THE RISK-AWARE CULTURE

Culture is a huge differentiator in the marketplace. If a bank is successful, its success is due mainly because of its culture. Since culture is built into a bank's very DNA, for any strategy to succeed, it must fit, or work within, that culture. Consequently, bank executives must design an ERM implementation strategy to complement their bank's culture, not compete with it. A good start is to make the bank team risk aware.

Making the Bank Culture Aware of Risk

The advent of modern risk management came with the calculation of probabilities, corresponding specifically with the growing popularity of gambling.[9] (The prospect of achieving wealth is irresistible for most people.) Taking risks and managing them has to do with taking stock, measuring the risk inherent in an opportunity. Do we take these steps? Can we afford to? Can we afford not to?

Calculating Probabilities

The engine behind ERM is that measurement leads to improved capabilities. It is important then, in making the culture risk aware, that the bank executive views ERM as a process. Any process can be measured, and with measurement comes the potential for improvement.

The problem with measurement, however, is that employees may become defensive, and a bank's culture may exacerbate that emotion. Employees who have practiced their craft over time will resist someone looking over their shoulder as they would a new hire. It is, therefore, important to first "type" the culture to find out what obstacles the bank executive must overcome to implement ERM.

TYPING THE CULTURE

What type of culture does your bank have? Is it risk averse, risk neutral, or risk tolerant?

When determining which of these characteristics describes your bank's culture, it is important to be objective. A common pitfall is to look at risk from one's own perspective, forgetting that the culture is the collective values of all of the people in the organization. In fact, a bank can "type" its culture by looking into the characteristics of its most successful people or even by using the "pig in the parlor" analogy discussed below.

The Most Successful People

What are the characteristics of the most successful people in the organization? A bank's culture is reflected in the values and behaviors of those people. Who gets the plum assignments? Who gets to rescue a failing initiative? Who gets an appointment with the CEO without going through line management? The list one develops is indicative of the organization's culture.[10] It will not overtly help the bank executive assess risk, but it should indicate whether the organization is risk tolerant, risk averse, or risk neutral. And that is a very good starting place in determining how big and far-reaching an ERM initiative will be.

How would a bank executive normally react to a proverbial pig in the parlor, the bank's main lobby? After all, pigs, on one hand, have been the subject of nursery rhymes and cartoons. Risk tolerant? On the other hand, pigs can appear to be big and disgusting creatures. Risk averse? If one were in the lobby, what would a banker do? Order it out, or what?

STRATEGIES FOR BUILDING RISK AWARENESS

Chances are that a bank executive will find himself in a risk-tolerant culture, particularly if the bank is successful. If the bank were not prepared to take risks, it would not open its doors in the morning. However, it remains important to type the culture to build ERM within its context and adjust the implementation strategy to fit it, as described below in detail and summarized in exhibit 2.1.

Risk-Averse Culture Strategies

A risk-averse culture will see ERM as a way to focus on the threats to the bank's business. Internal communication should zoom in on corporate scandals such as those that occurred at Allied Irish and Barings (rogue brokers), on well-publicized regulation violations (for example, SARs filings, BSA/AML issues) at Riggs and AmSouth banks, on capital deficiencies, or on the

EXHIBIT 2.1 Value-Added Strategies for Company Buy-In, by Culture Type

	Risk-Averse Culture	Risk-Neutral Culture	Risk-Tolerant Culture
Value-Added Strategies	➤ Remove or neutralize a threat. ➤ Add controls and measures. ➤ Regularly report on the ERM initiative. ➤ Elevate the roles of Internal Audit and Compliance within the organization.	➤ Prove that ERM is not a regulatory exercise but a business strategy. ➤ Connect ERM not only with SOX, GLBA, and FDICIA, but also with everything else the company does: business decisions, new products and services, hiring key executives, and so forth.	➤ Find the competitive advantages and economic incentives ERM brings to the organization. ➤ Design systems that will keep regulatory agencies and corporate insurers comfortable. ➤ Show how more sophisticated approaches to managing risks will delight shareholders, ratings agencies, and Wall Street.

bank's own internal and external exam findings. All of the strategies to push ERM throughout the culture should center on:

- removing or neutralizing a threat
- adding controls and measures
- reporting regularly on the ERM initiative
- elevating the roles of internal audit and compliance within the organization

In a risk-averse organization, the "pig in the parlor" would be driven out immediately and at all costs. A word of caution: in a risk-averse organization, people may see a pig when there is no pig, or they might see something as an undesired pig when, in actuality, it might be something very desirable.

Risk-Neutral Culture Strategies

A risk-neutral culture is not as quick to move on a real or perceived threat. It would take the posture: is a pig a bad thing? It might work well within the organization. Can we form a task force to find out? Is the pig something we can live with? What if the CEO likes the pig (i.e., sees it as something desirable for the organization)?

ERM strategies in a risk-neutral company are a bit more challenging. The bank executive must make the ERM initiative about:

- proving that ERM is not a regulatory exercise but a business strategy (see chapter 1)
- connecting ERM not only with SOX, GLBA, and FDICIA, but also with everything else the company does: business decisions, new products and services, hiring key executives, and so forth

Risk-Tolerant Culture Strategies

A risk-tolerant culture presents the biggest challenge of all: it may not see the pig. In this case, bank executives should forget selling ERM on the basis of threats to the organization and turn their attention to:

- finding the competitive advantages and economic incentives ERM brings to the organization
- designing systems that will keep regulatory agencies and corporate insurers comfortable
- taking the opportunity to show how more sophisticated approaches to managing risks will delight shareholders, ratings agencies, and Wall Street

A summary of these strategies appears in exhibit 2.1.

COMMITMENT FROM THE TOP

Gaining CEO commitment and executive management buy-in is essential to the success of any corporate-wide initiative. Executive management support helps the sponsor of the initiative to mobilize the entire organization toward the goal, a process that is difficult in and of itself and cannot otherwise be achieved.

This is particularly true for the bank executive turned enterprise risk manager. Since it rarely has a large support staff, the job is extremely challenging. The enterprise risk manager typically has responsibility but not direct resources. Management by influence is the cornerstone for success, and the CEO's blessing is essential to achieve the credibility to build influence.

The challenge faced by executives responsible for ERM is even greater, since other managers oversee many of the risks with which the ERM bank executive also is mantled. Each one of those managers has infrastructure to support him, as well as the responsibility for the day-to-day management of the risks under his control (for example, credit, interest rate, market, operational, and so forth). The executives who run these respective departments often perceive the ERM bank executive as a usurper, someone who is looking at their work to find flaws, a threat that needs to be managed. They fail to see the added value that an enterprise-wide view brings to the table, as well as the overall portfolio approach to risk. The challenge associated with such an attitude is huge, since these departmental managers control the necessary resources for their respective risk management, as well as the flow of information about the risks that they manage. Both attitude and information are key to the ERM bank executives' accurate assessment of the corporate-wide risk profile and their ability to execute risk optimization across departments and lines of business.

More Overhead or Value-Added?

For the CEO making the decision to add ERM to his or her own duties, finding the value-added proposition is not an issue; he or she already has found it. But what should a newly appointed ERM bank executive do to obtain the necessary buy-in from both the CEO and the executive suite, as well as from other risk managers within the organization, if the support is not already there? Demonstrating the value added to the organization by their presence and vantage point is the answer. An ERM bank executive may be viewed either as unnecessary overhead or as an essential strategic partner to all lines of business and executive management.

The CEO and the other managers must see the ERM bank executive as someone who helps them perform their jobs better. It is critical that the ERM executive view other managers as clients and vital collaborators to be won over, not as competitors or obstacles to success. Treating them as prospective customers changes not only the ERM manager's behavior, but also the customers' view of the ERM manager, for the better.

Clients and Collaborators

The first person on this list is the CEO, and the list includes all heads of lines of business as well as the risk functions within the bank.[11] The simple question is: what's in it for them? Several thoughts:

First, at the corporate level, effective risk management goes well beyond any individual risk. Corporate ERM looks at the portfolio of risks the bank incurs and assesses the interaction among them. As a result, risk might be reduced because two lines of business could counteract each other. A classic example is mortgage origination and servicing. Clearly, these two businesses are counter-cyclical; when one is doing well, the other is suffering. While their dual presence already is considered an interest-rate risk-reduction tool, there are other, similarly positive implications for capital requirements, organization-wide profitability, and other elements. Examining all lines of business together as a single portfolio to determine which ones create additional risk through their mutual presence and which ones reduce risk as pairs or other combinations is the sole purview of the ERM bank executive. Everyone in the organization can learn from a demonstration of how to reduce various risks by considering them together instead of as a stand-alone issue. This knowledge is valuable to all business owners as well as the CEO, and the ERM executive is the only person in the bank who can take the gestalt view—seeing all the risks in all lines of business in a unified whole.

Second, demonstrate reliance on existing risk managers and their resources. As a professional with limited resources, the executive assigned to oversee enterprise risk management relies on the existing infrastructure for information, ideas, and brainstorming. The successful ERM bank executive does not compete with the various risk managers. Instead, he or she accepts them as equal partners. The organization will cooperate if the executive in the enterprise management position becomes the warehouse of enterprise-wide risk information and not the owner and manager of the risks themselves. In other words, the ERM bank executive is not there to criticize and second-guess existing conclusions, but to use the information in a different, much more strategic context.

Third, provide analytics that are currently missing from the executive table to facilitate sounder decision making. Few organizations truly consider the full range of risks—which, depending on the size and scope of the business, could number in the hundreds—in making decisions, mainly because it is difficult to expand the view outside of individual lines of business. The ERM bank executive has a unique opportunity to add this dimension to the executive table by producing a unique analysis of information provided by others to highlight the tradeoffs the company is making with and without full consideration of the risks. For example, is capital allocation to all businesses reflective of the risks embedded in those businesses? The ERM bank executive can lead the executive team in recognizing the differences across businesses and allocating capital properly to yield true and effective risk-based decisions. He or she can add the risk dimension to strategic business discussions that currently are missing that element. For example, diversification across businesses rarely is considered when lines of business are evaluated for expansion, additional investment, or contraction. Each decision is viewed as a stand-alone tactic. In reality, there are risk reduction benefits to building revenue streams across lines of business that might not be taken into account in the discussion. The ERM bank executive can add that dimension to the team.

Finally, add the risk analytics to presentations to investors. Analysts are getting more and more concerned with companies' risk profiles and their self-awareness of their situation. The ERM bank executive can help the CEO and CFO improve investor relations by adding just a couple of slides to their show, illustrating the incorporation of the risk element into the company's decision making and information dissemination. Analysts are not looking for risk avoidance; they are looking for risk awareness. Who better than the ERM bank executive to provide that component to outside audiences?

Back Seat or Driving Force?

The CEO's endorsement of the ERM function in the bank is, as mentioned, an essential element in building the credibility and sphere of influence of the ERM bank executive. The CEO needs to recognize, publicly and repeatedly, the value of the function and voice his or her expectation of intracompany collaboration. This action will improve the company's risk profile under the ERM bank executive's leadership. The CEO will only do so if he or she feels the function truly provides value and that the ERM bank executive can contribute to the quality and profitability of decision making at the highest levels.

Toward that end, think about the decisions and corporate-wide risk management issues from the CEO and CFO's vantage point rather than from the auditors' or the other risk managers'. Learn *their* definition of success for the ERM function. Starting from their definition of success will prevent the ERM bank executive from looking at the function from his own personal perspective only and will help him become more effective. Different CEOs have different visions for ERM, which often reflect their management philosophy. Transplanting a "perfect" ERM plan into the company might be a noble ambition, but if the plan does not fit the culture, it is doomed to fail. Tailoring the approach, staffing the ERM position and integrating ERM into the CEO's specific vision and the company's culture will facilitate success for the ERM bank executive and the value he or she can bring to all constituencies.

For example, some companies are highly analytical. A quantitative approach to risk management and reports that fit the company's overall format will enhance the ERM executive's credibility and help integrate the ERM function effectively into the bank. However, when the CEO's management style is more "from the heart," producing reams of reports would only distance the ERM bank executive from the focus of management, thus separating ERM from the rest of the bank. In that case, the

ERM executive fares better using persuasive and team-based methods of management. Knowing the company's culture and fitting into it are important ingredients to success.

The ERM bank executive can dispel a CEO's skepticism of the risk management function by:

- effectively considering the riskiness associated with different ventures
- adding value without increasing cost significantly
- working with others within the organization

The Board of Directors

After Sarbanes-Oxley and the amendments to the U.S. Sentencing Guidelines, the bank executive is finding a more engaged and better-informed board of directors. The bank's culture also will dictate how the board responds to ERM. There are many schools of thought about reporting responsibility, but overall, there are two broad choices: the ERM function reports either to the entire board or to a board committee. The selection should be based on whether senior management wants the entire board thinking about ERM *part* of the time, or a board committee thinking about it *all* of the time.

If a bank chooses to have the ERM function report to a board committee, there are two choices here, too. The ERM function can report to an existing committee or to a committee dedicated only to ERM. The problem with the former is that members of an existing board committee already have a particular function. A dedicated ERM committee may dilute the existing committee's effect on the organization. Additionally, having ERM report to an existing board committee may send a message the bank does not wish to send—that ERM is an audit or corporate governance function. Creating a separate ERM board committee, however, can be costly and perpetuate an attitude that ERM is a "siloed," not an enterprise, function.

CONCLUSION

There are many paths through which a bank can develop an organizational ERM program. Each has its own pitfalls as well as opportunities. One thing is clear, however. ERM cannot survive in a vacuum. Its success or failure is determined by how well it fits and works with the culture of the company.

Key Points
ERM and the Bank's Culture

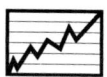

- It is important to determine whether the bank is risk averse, risk neutral, or risk tolerant; tailor the strategies for adoption of ERM to that determination.
- Integral to any ERM effort is the buy-in at the top of the organization as well as throughout management.
- The ERM bank executive should be seen as a collaborator and an aide to the business line. A risk manager should not be seen as a hindrance or usurper, or as unnecessary overhead.

Chapter 3

CREATING THE PROPER INFRASTRUCTURE TO MAXIMIZE ERM

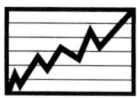

A smart man learns from his own mistakes, a wise man learns from the mistakes of others, and a fool never learns.
Chinese Proverb

The Tao of Risk Management. Tao means "way, road, or path." To Taoists, the harmony and orderliness perceived in the universe are manifestations of a divine will or legislation existing and regulating the universe. Taoism, in its basic form, is the idea that everything will come out right if people sit back, do nothing, and let nature take its course.

Risk management is the antithesis of Taoism. Risk management actively seeks to identify, assess, and manage risks. In this effort, banks hire risk managers, reorganize entire departments, develop policies and procedures, and seek to integrate risk management throughout the company.

Unfortunately, some bankers still believe risk management is a fad, that their institution cannot or will not reap benefits from ERM, or that implementation of ERM is too costly and difficult. Cynics such as these will sit back and do nothing, and nature WILL eventually take its course.

Formula for Success

No standardized organizational structure exists for risk management. The appropriate structure must be considered in terms of the size and complexity of the bank, the expectations of all stakeholders, the bank's overall corporate culture, and most importantly, the tone at the top. The bank executive will be successful:

- ➤ once management perceives the risk management function as a partner in achieving strategic, operational, and financial objectives, and promotes risk management
- ➤ once he or she is knowledgeable about the various options for coordination and collaboration of an internal audit with ERM

This chapter discusses traditional and evolving risk management departmental structures and the need to balance independence with participation in strategic management of the bank. In general, the structure must conform to the bank's strategic goals and to risk policies established by the board of directors. And it must incorporate the role of internal audit. Both line managers and senior managers also must understand the bank's risk profile, the board's risk appetite, and the role of the chief risk officer.

THE CHALLENGE OF ERM

Without a doubt, financial management and enterprise risk management are interconnected, even though most companies continue to treat them as independent disciplines. Obviously, financial consequences accompany every risk and, likewise, every financial strategy begets its own risks.

Many companies also will associate risk management with corporate governance, and often these companies will possess highly developed risk management and risk-reporting structures.

Banking regulators, indeed, the industry itself, increasingly insist on bank's developing and implementing more robust risk management processes. Boards are adopting risk management policies that outline risk assessment and governance processes, organizational structure with board oversight, and management's responsibilities and then designating a senior executive to be responsible for enterprise risk management.

These policies and processes provide a way to define risk assessment and reporting standards, encourage enhancements to existing practices, and facilitate thoughtful and deliberate movement into new areas of risk management. When coupled with the appropriate resources, these policy changes can have a very rapid and positive effect on a bank's risk profile. The challenge to the board is to use these resources skillfully for the benefit of the bank and its stakeholders.

FUNCTIONING ERM

Every employee of a bank is a risk manager. All employees, therefore, must thoughtfully consider the potential severity of the risks they face daily. In addition, they must consider the overall impact of their decisions on other business units, in the context of the risk appetite established by the bank's board and senior management. In this sense, risk management no longer focuses on *my* risks but rather on *our* risks.

So what are the essential responsibilities of the ERM function? As risk management evolves within the company, its responsibilities obviously will change. Nevertheless, fundamentally, the principal responsibilities include:

- serving as an organizing body for various risk management activities throughout the organization
- acting in collaboration with management as a consultant and resource
- identifying and assessing risk
- developing and managing a comprehensive, fully integrated, strategic risk management plan
- acting as the company's principal assessor and manager of economic capital and shareholder value

Risk management does not have to be complex; in fact, it is most effective when it is straightforward and well defined. All banks certainly will benefit from adopting a formal risk management function. Though larger banks will need to adopt sophisticated models and hire a department of quantitative analysts ("quants"), smaller banks can use simpler means to achieve the same benefits, as this book explains. Most importantly, a successful risk management program must be tailored to the specific needs of the organization.

To establish an effective ERM program, banks must use fundamental ERM guidelines. They must apply an integrated process that examines the bank's risks across all business lines, allocates appropriate resources, and participates in strategic planning at the most senior levels.

A board of directors must clearly define risk management's objectives, organizational structure, and implementation plan. The board and management, at all levels, also must define certain risk benchmarks and other measures of accomplishment. The ultimate effectiveness of any risk management program is not measured by the size of its policies or its organizational structure but rather by the fulfillment of the promise that risk management is a strategic business decision that will add real economic value to the company. Therefore, a more complete definition of risk management is that it is a discipline that attempts to create and protect shareholder value. It does this not only by mitigating threats but also by exploiting opportunities.

THE APPROPRIATE STRUCTURE

As for organizational integration, the emerging best practice suggests that the chief risk officer (CRO) be a senior executive of the company. It is neither practical nor effective to regard the CRO as an extension of traditional risk management (for example, corporate insurance, internal audit, compliance) or financial management. Unfortunately, many institutions mistakenly embed ERM within those functions.

To develop an ERM program, one of the first steps a bank should take is consolidate some of the bank's more traditional risk-assessment functions and link group risk with the bank's various business areas. If the bank has a holding company, the ERM function must be recentralized within the holding company. The primary goals of the structural aspects of risk management are to: (1) create a risk-aware culture, (2) bring the consideration of risk into strategic decision making, (3) develop and exploit the expertise of highly skilled individual risk managers, and (4) communicate to stakeholders and be an advisor to other executives and managers.

The most effective structural model emerging in the industry consists of a risk management division comprised of loan review (credit risk), compliance (regulatory risk), market risk, and operational risk, in coordination with internal audit (more on this later). Each function is responsible for risk services to every line of business and to each of the bank's affiliates.

For smaller institutions, this structure may not be as easy to develop. However, the bank may find that it can outsource the assessment of certain risks (and usually pay a premium) until it can develop its own resources and intellectual capital.

The advantages of a fully integrated ERM structure should be intuitive. Such a structure makes it possible for managers in all business units to identify, assess, and manage risks across each line of business, their operation, and their business strategy. It also helps managers comprehend the influences particular risks have on one another and directs management's attention to more global risk management strategies.

Risk Silos versus Enterprise Risk Management

Managing risk in terms of individual risk silos is an acceptable first step toward developing a fully integrated ERM function. However, management and the board must understand that individual risk silos have limitations. The most significant limitation is that siloed risk management views risks within each business unit in isolation, without considering interrelationships with other risks within other areas of the company.

Banking regulators, industry analysts, and indeed, some long-time risk practitioners continue to tolerate a siloed approach. However, they have never been happy with it. In contrast, a fully integrated ERM function considers risks during the bank's strategic planning process as well as in day-to-day operations. This set-up obliges senior management to assess how much risk the bank is prepared to accept. It also demands that risk management be conducted outside of individual risk silos and instead through a more holistic, fully integrated view of risks across various lines of business.

ERM transcends departmental functions, cutting across all lines of business and activities of the company. Understanding that risks in one area of the bank affect other business units and the company as a whole is central to understanding ERM. For this reason, as will be discussed shortly, it is important to designate a central risk authority, someone to coordinate the company's various risk-assessment processes and implement the company's risk management plan.

For example, a mortgage loan may expose the bank to both credit risk and interest-rate risk. If the mortgage is not appropriately filed or documented, the bank has further encountered an operational risk.

One of the more significant impediments to establishing an ERM function is, ironically, the interrelationship of risks among each other. These relationships may be difficult to monitor and quantify. They are, nevertheless, very important to understand and may significantly dictate the effectiveness of an ERM program.

Despite this hurdle, an increasing number of banks have already begun to develop a fully integrated ERM program in order to assess and manage risks on a more integrated basis, across all lines of business, and reporting upward under the leadership of a single chief risk officer (see exhibit 3.1).

EXHIBIT 3.1 The Advantages of a Fully-Integrated Risk Management Model

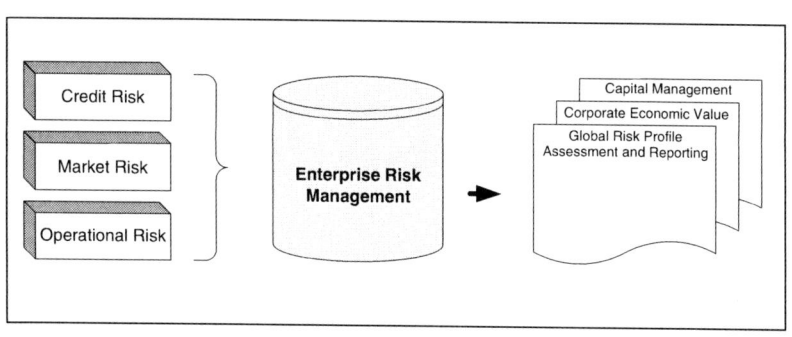

ERM Benefits

In placing emphasis on the ERM function, and restructuring the bank to support it, some obvious benefits of ERM emerge:

- It establishes ownership for inherent risks at each line of business. It never "owns" the risk. Rather, it identifies, measures, assesses, and helps manage risk.
- It aligns risks, across the entire enterprise, to the bank's strategic objectives.
- It helps predict catastrophic risk events so that management can plan beforehand and spend less time "fighting fires" when they arise.
- It enhances identification and assessment of risks on a global basis, enabling senior management to make risk-based decisions.

Applying an ERM process demands a common understanding of risks and the bank's risk tolerances, particularly at the senior management and board levels. The bank's risk management department assesses and monitors risks across lines of business (and in some cases, it will manage the risks) and reports on the success of various risk management efforts management employs throughout the organization. It is important for risk managers to understand that they should focus on risk *effects* when assessing risk and on risk *events* when managing risk.

For this reason, it is important to designate a central risk authority, someone to coordinate the company's various risk-assessment processes and implement the company's risk management plan.

ROLE OF THE RISK MANAGEMENT FUNCTION

Risk management has evolved well beyond the traditional confines of compliance or audit. For example, in an effort to assess and manage credit risk, banks traditionally relied on a loan-review function. Today, however, assessing credit risk has evolved well beyond a continuous review of credit files and traditional credit reports. A robust credit risk assessment function today includes:

- estimations of when loan defaults may occur
- loan default probabilities
- estimated losses, assuming a credit default
- risk-adjusted returns on equity
- allocations of economic capital

Similarly, many bank compliance departments are being integrated into a more robust regulatory risk department that not only ensures the bank remains in compliance with consumer lending and deposit regulations, but also ensures the bank remains in compliance with a host of other SEC and NASDAQ regulations and Acts of Congress that directly or indirectly affect the bank. In essence, regulatory risk has become one-stop shopping for all the bank's compliance needs. Furthermore, rather than act solely as an audit or police unit, regulatory risk departments also assess the origins of compliance failures, act as consultants and suggest changes where needed, conduct training, and generally integrate themselves into the bank's senior management and committee structures.

Traditional asset and liability modeling is, to some degree, being supplanted by more robust market risk economic capital models. Where operational risk traditionally has been relegated to focusing on fraud and security, operational risk assessment is now one of the fastest growing quantitative and qualitative areas in banking. It is used to measure the frequency and severity of transaction or process failures (see chapter 6).

Regardless of the structure, the role of the risk management function should include:

- developing and executing risk management policies and processes
- developing a strategic vision for the bank's risk management program

- organizing the myriad functional activities throughout the bank that report on risk management issues
- preparing various reports for the board of directors, other senior managers, and stakeholders
- participating as a senior executive in the bank's strategic planning, financial reporting, and day-to-day operations
- becoming the bank's ambassador for risk management and establishing a risk-conscious culture

In short, the goal of the risk management function should be to develop an integrated risk management model that:

- incorporates all risk elements
- prioritizes risk as high, moderate, or low
- trends the risks as increasing, decreasing, or stable
- measures risks in quantitative terms such as economic capital, value-at-risk, and risk-adjusted returns on equity
- includes qualitative measures such as experience and intuition

THE ROLE OF THE CHIEF RISK OFFICER

Every employee is a risk manager. However, without a centralized risk officer, the understanding of risks, their influences across multiple lines of business, and the alignment of risks into the bank's overall objectives is virtually impossible. For this reason, it is imperative that banks appoint a risk coordinator, a chief risk officer (CRO), to assess (and, if necessary, direct) the various risk management efforts undertaken across the enterprise. The CRO is responsible for assessing, developing, and directing risk management strategy and for exploiting risk management opportunities to help the bank realize its business goals.

Some banks have placed designated risk officers throughout the company, within various lines of business. While this strategy will facilitate managing risks within each of the specific business lines, the obvious shortcoming is that it impedes the coordinated management of risk across the enterprise. For this reason too, appointing a CRO is essential. A CRO will not eliminate the need for risk managers elsewhere in the company. Rather, he or she will formalize an integrated approach to risk management.

Responsibilities

With the help of an effective risk management staff, the chief risk officer is responsible for:

- identifying the most significant risks the bank faces
- assigning a value to a given risk level, either quantitatively or qualitatively
- assessing and reporting on changes in the level and trends of risk over time; in more mature programs, risk will be reported against a capital limit or other benchmark
- directing risk management to comply with the risk-taking appetite and policies set by shareholders and board of directors

Risk management may take many forms, and it is up to the CRO to determine which risk management strategies will be most effective. Management and the board must understand that usually the summary elimination of risks is very costly, if not impossible. While it is understood that banks are in the business of taking risks, it is the management of those risks that is central to the risk management process. Typically, the CRO is responsible for assessing and directing the process.

In a manner of speaking, the CRO acts as a symphony conductor. He or she must be able to communicate and lead the discussion and interchange among managers. The CRO must assess and interpret risk reports from various sources and lead, guide, and direct the bank's management staff in managing those risks. As a matter of interpretation, the CRO bears ultimate responsibility for the effectiveness of the risk management function, and, therefore, must have the final word on the interpretation of risk data, including reporting risk levels and the effectiveness of risk management techniques.

For the CRO to succeed, he or she must have the absolute support of the board and senior management. Without this support, the CRO is destined to fail. For the CRO to succeed in meeting the needs of the board and overcome organizational resistance, he or she also must adopt the role of leader, facilitator, negotiator, and ambassador.

The Need for Independence

For any risk management program to succeed, risk managers and indeed the CRO must be independent of risk-taking functions within the bank. This independence is achieved via the following criteria:[12]

- Risk managers reporting lines must be independent from risk-taking functions.
- Except at the highest levels, risk takers must have no input on the performance reviews, compensation, or promotion of risk managers, and conversely.
- Employees cannot be risk takers and simultaneously be assessors of the same risks.

Federal Reserve Governor Susan Schmidt Bies, at the International Center for Business Information's Risk Management 2004 Conference in Geneva, Switzerland, stated that "one weakness we have seen is the delegation by management of both the development and the assessment of the internal-control structure to the same risk management, internal-control, or compliance group. It is important to emphasize that line management has the responsibility for identifying risks and ensuring that the mitigating controls are effective—and to leave the assessments to a group that is independent of that line organization."[13]

So, with the importance of independence confirmed by the Federal Reserve and others, the question then becomes, to whom will the CRO and ERM function report? Present practice reveals two predominant reporting lines for the ERM function. The CRO frequently reports directly to either the CEO or to the board of directors. However, emerging practices reveal a dual reporting relationship where the CRO reports to *both* the CEO *and* the board of directors (or to the board's audit or ERM committee). This dual reporting structure is required largely as a result of a bank's ERM's structure rather than the emerging importance of the ERM function.

As previously discussed, a fully integrated ERM structure will consist of various departments, including credit risk, regulatory risk, internal audit, and others, all of which require a degree of independence from management and direct reporting to the board of directors. This independence, if not intuitive, is nevertheless required by federal and many state banking regulators.

For example, the Federal Reserve and the Comptroller of the Currency, who have issued various opinions on the matter, expect the credit-risk function to be independent. In fact, the comptroller's handbook explicitly states that the loan review function should report directly to the board of directors, which "approves the unit's operating budget, prepares the performance evaluation for the division's head, approves the unit's strategic and operating plans, acts on the unit's findings, and ratifies administrative matters."[14]

Likewise, with the bank compliance function, banking regulators insist that the bank's compliance officers should present his or her reports directly to the bank's board of directors.[15] To further add to the compliance officer's need for independence, most compliance departments also are responsible for assessing the adequacy of the bank's Bank Secrecy Act (BSA) program. A critical component to any BSA program is independent testing for compliance. Again, banking industry regulators, as well as audit firms and other industry pundits, have published various articles on the need for independent compliance testing.

Consequently, bank boards are faced with either having to supervise several risk managers or to name one risk spokesman, a chief risk officer, to manage and report on all aspects of risk within the company.

Finally, in an interagency policy statement published in 2003, the four principal federal banking regulators (Federal Reserve, OCC, OTS, and FDIC) state that "some institutions seek to coordinate the internal audit function with several risk monitoring functions (for example, loan review, market risk assessment, and legal compliance departments) by establishing an administrative arrangement under one senior executive. Coordination of these other monitoring activities can facilitate the reporting of material risk and control issues to the audit committee, increase the overall effectiveness of these monitoring functions, better utilize available resources, and enhance the institution's ability to comprehensively manage risk." The statement also cautions that "such an administrative reporting relationship should be designed so as to not interfere with or hinder the manager of internal audit's functional reporting to and ability to directly communicate with the institution's audit committee."[16]

THE ROLE OF INTERNAL AUDIT IN ERM

In God we trust. Everyone else we audit.
Audit Axiom Number One

The past decade witnessed an upsurge in the frequency, scope, and responsibilities of the internal audit process. Reasons for this significant increase include high-profile corporate failures, a decline in the trust of corporate boards and management, an increase in corporate complexity, and increased sensitivity to risk versus reward.

When considering internal audit in its purest form, there is a well-defined relationship between audit and confidence. An emerging view, however, is that internal audit should be integrated into ERM. When integrated into a risk management program, internal audit and its assessment of internal controls become in some respects the foundation on which a robust ERM program is built. Separating ERM and audit functions invites duplication of effort, inconsistencies, overlaps, and increased costs; fully intertwining the two leads to possible loss of independence.

While COSO falls short of directly encouraging the integration of internal audit into ERM, it does profess that its recently published enterprise risk management framework is much broader than its internal control framework and, in fact, incorporates the internal control framework within it. Furthermore, the COSO model suggests that an effective ERM function is a strategic business function, not merely a control or "police" function.

The Institute of Internal Auditors (IIA), the premier authoritative body for internal audit practices, suggests that internal audit take a consultative role in the ERM process.[17] In fact, the IIA calls identifying and evaluating risks, coaching management in responding to risks, and developing risk management strategy "legitimate internal-auditing roles with safeguards."[18] Finally, the IIA asserts that the internal-audit function helps management "accomplish its objectives by bringing a systematic, disciplined approach to evaluate and improve the effectiveness of risk management, control, and governance processes."[19] The danger here is that the internal-audit function easily can become a *de facto* ERM function. In addition, the IIA concept places internal audit on a slippery slope to losing its independence. If this concept were to become accepted practice, ERM would become an audit or control function rather than a strategic management function.

If the audit industry and other theorists of risk management promote internal audit's consultative role, that is, its involvement in establishing risk management methodologies, benchmarks, and strategies, the key role of internal audit gets lost. If internal audit loses its primarily responsibility—to ensure that the numbers reported by the company are accurate—who is minding the books? Following the collapse of Enron and other cataclysmic accounting irregularities by other large corporations, the most noteworthy lesson for banks and their shareholders is that the internal audit function should return to its basic and most valuable role—impartially evaluating the accuracy of the bank's financial records and internal controls.

Although the internal audit function generally is relegated to ensuring the accuracy of financial reporting and the effectiveness of internal controls, the risk management function is truly a management function. It includes consulting, strategic planning, and managing the institution. Internal auditors should not make risk management decisions.

Nevertheless, the bank's internal auditors traditionally have held the reigns of a pseudo risk management function, focusing on a myriad of qualitative assessments of internal controls. Today, risk management is far more complex: it requires qualitative *and* quantitative processes, and it depends on the successful integration of ERM into the bank's management.

Recently, there has been much debate about the reporting structure of an internal audit function. If an internal audit function must be purely independent and objective, then the reporting structure becomes more apparent: internal audit must report directly to the board audit committee. From a logistical perspective, a dual-reporting structure works much more effectively for internal-audit functions. In this structure, the chief internal auditor reports *functionally* to the board audit committee and *administratively* to the CEO.[20]

How does internal audit fit within ERM? One thing is certain, the internal audit function should not manage ERM. Specifically, it should *not* set the risk appetite of the bank, own the bank's internal controls, or create bank policies and procedures for functions other than internal audit. However, to suggest that a "Chinese Wall" separates the internal audit function from the risk management function also is misguided. In fact, the two functions must work collaboratively with one another. In many ways, the successful execution of the bank's risk management efforts, particularly operational risk, relies on an adequate system of internal controls. In this case, an unseen but very real umbilical cord ties the two together.

For this reason, as they develop risk management functions, more and more banks are moving the internal audit function under the risk management umbrella and, consequently, integrating the internal-audit function into ERM. As more banks adopt ERM, the internal auditor's reporting lines are shifting away from the board of directors and toward the chief risk officer. For evidence of this, one has only to look at the recent appointment and responsibilities of chief risk officers at some of the nation's well respected banks (Washington Mutual Inc., PNC Financial Services, AmSouth Bank, Commerce Bancorp (New Jersey), City National Bank (California)). But does this reporting structure automatically compromise the independence of the internal-audit function? The answer, as will be discussed in a moment, is no.

As risk management processes evolve, internal auditors are finding their role in risk management decreasing. Conversely, with respect to financial reporting risks, the role of the internal auditor is again flourishing. Particularly for publicly traded banks, the financial-reporting risks associated with compliance with Section 404 of the Sarbanes-Oxley Act can be very high. In this case, relying on an effective internal audit function is critical because successful compliance with the Act (both an operational and regulatory risk) is grounded on management having established an adequate system of internal controls. Again, whereas risk management as a whole is more of an analytical, consultative, and strategic management function—and therefore not typically equipped to assess internal controls—the internal auditor is the assessor of internal controls and an integral part of ERM.

Precisely for this reason, in 2003 the four principal federal banking regulators issued an interagency policy statement addressing the real-world practicalities of ERM. In that statement, all four banking regulators acknowledged that as the field of ERM has developed some banks have found it preferable (if not more effective) to integrate internal audit into risk management. Specifically, the policy statement says:

> some institutions seek to coordinate the internal audit function with several risk monitoring functions (e.g., loan review, market risk assessment, and legal compliance departments) by establishing an administrative arrangement under one senior executive. Coordination of these other monitoring activities can facilitate the reporting of material risk and control issues to the audit committee, increase the overall effectiveness of these monitoring functions, better utilize available resources, and enhance the institution's ability to comprehensively manage risk.[21]

This arrangement is acceptable as long as the risk management function, indeed, the chief risk officer, has an unrestricted ability to report to the board of directors or to a board committee.

HIRING OR ASSIGNING A FULL-TIME CHIEF RISK OFFICER

The ERM program must include a central "risk czar" whose sole responsibility is to aggregate and assess risks from throughout the company. This is a big job. The chief risk officer's duties cannot be split along other functions such as audit, lending, or finance.

The qualifications necessary for an effective chief risk officer (CRO) largely depend on the structure and complexity of the bank. How important is prior risk management experience? A purely quantitative (mathematical, statistical, or economic) approach to ERM would not be served well by extensive hands-on risk management experience. On the other hand, a more qualitative approach, one that relies on intuition and judgment as well as mathematical analysis, will benefit a great deal from a CRO with extensive hands-on risk management experience.

The risk manager may find it difficult to persuade management, indeed, all stakeholders, about excessive risk, particularly when quantitative processes do not exist. Differences in judgment are difficult to resolve. For this reason, there is no substitute for experience and credibility.

The Qualified CRO

What should the bank executive look for in a CRO? The CRO candidate must be experienced in assessing and managing various forms of risk. Since credit and market risk are typically considered to be the most significant risks facing any financial institution, the CRO should have a strong background in these functions. (See a CRO job description in appendix A.)

Experience is not always enough, however. The CRO also must be an ambassador for ERM. By developing a collaborative relationship with all stakeholders (directors, managers, employees), a CRO must be able to overcome the misconception that ERM is a police or audit function.

Finding the CRO

Where does bank management look for a CRO? Because ERM is relatively new to banking in the United States, experienced CROs are difficult to find. To begin the search, the board should consider:

- risk managers from other institutions
- bank regulators
- risk management consultants

Risk Managers from Other Institutions. Larger banking institutions may employ several mid- and senior-level risk managers that would welcome the opportunity to direct the risk management function at a smaller institution. Under the guidance of a CRO, these risk managers often have become skilled at ERM, risk analysis, reporting, collaborating with stakeholders, and meeting with senior managers and the board. Often, they act as liaisons with the bank's regulators. They are a good resource for smaller banks to hire.

The smallest banks, however, may not feel they can afford to hire a person with the experience and expertise required of a CRO. These institutions might consider appointing a CRO from within their organization. And because credit risk is always the most significant risk facing smaller banking institutions, the board could consider delegating the risk management function to a credit manager having a strong background in loan review, credit policy and administration, and loan operations. The CRO position is a full-time position, and *the CRO's responsibilities should not be divided among risk management and other operational areas of the bank.*

Bank Regulators. Bank regulators are solidly trained as risk assessors, and senior bank examiners with many years of experience and expertise in various types of risks might be excellent candidates for the CRO position. Generally, "commissioned" or "certified" bank examiners have at least several years experience as risk assessors. All have had to pass a very comprehensive examination attesting to their skills in credit, operations, compliance, market risk, asset/liability management, and audit to demonstrate their expertise. A residual benefit to hiring a bank examiner to lead the risk management function is that bank examiners have first-hand knowledge of regulatory expectations about the function as well as exceptional resources.

Risk Management Consultants. In the past few years, many risk management consulting firms, both large and small, have jumped into ERM consulting for banks, utilities firms, and a few other industries. Many of them would like the chance to implement ERM programs rather than to consult on them. If you are already working with such a consulting firm, you may already have met your first CRO.

For small banks, knowing where *not* to look is as important as knowing where to look. As a general rule, in banks of all sizes, neither auditors nor finance analysts possess the skill sets necessary to be an effective CRO.

Places to Avoid

Internal audit—though part of ERM—is *not* ERM. The skill set for success in the audit function is not the same for that in the ERM function. When management asks an internal auditor to perform a risk assessment of credit or treasury management, does either of them really know where to begin? Typically, no! The auditor can assess compliance with policies, procedures, and internal controls but typically cannot assess asset quality or the resulting adequacy of the bank's loan loss reserves.

A further danger is that if ERM emerges out of audit, ERM becomes an audit exercise, not a conduit of risk management or added shareholder value. The same holds true for other disciplines, and selecting a CRO from among them creates a source of confusion about the CRO's role within the organization. The CRO represents change, change that can be met either with resistance from other business units or with misdirection from the CEO. The latter guarantees ineffectiveness, especially when the CRO becomes the regulatory compliance officer, is expected to manage earnings, or becomes steeped in investor relations.[22]

Minimizing the Confusion: The CRO's Scorecard

CROs hold the unique position of keeping a company focused on risk, in a world where return is the overriding objective.

Eric Banfield in "Escalating Risk Visibility"

The CRO elevates the visibility of risk and brings a risk perspective to the bank's strategy.[23] Periodically, but no less than once per quarter, the bank's board and CEO should use the following scorecard (exhibit 3.2) to evaluate the CRO's performance (adapted from "Escalating Risk Visibility" by Eric Banfield for RiskCenter.com).

THE ROLE OF THE BOARD

The board of directors has an oversight role to determine that appropriate risk management processes are in place and that these processes are adequate and effective. Federal regulators also have published numerous documents on risk management and board oversight. Notwithstanding regulatory guidance, board members must understand the key elements of ERM, question management about risks, and approve certain strategic risk decisions. Nevertheless, because the board should not make decisions on behalf of management, management cannot delegate its role in risk management to the board of directors.

Delegation to a Board Committee

Many bank boards delegate oversight of the ERM process to either the audit committee or to an ERM committee. As a result, the designated committee has taken on renewed importance, and its input is now more significant than ever before. To meet analysts' earnings expectations, the committee should be particularly sensitive to both internal and external pressures when

EXHIBIT 3.2 The CRO's Scorecard

Discipline	CRO's Task
Strategy	Brings the risk perspective to strategic and financial decision making
Risk appetite	Ensures that executive management and the board define the bank's risk tolerance and appetite
Risk awareness	Widely communicates the bank's risk culture, attitude, and mentality
Risk framework	Works with all business groups to agree on a risk framework for the bank
Risk owner identification	Ensures that risk owners are identified and that they understand the risks they own
Risk management incentives	Provides incentives for risk owners to properly manage their risks
Risk aggregation	Standardizes, integrates, and aggregates all risks and elevates risk visibility
Risk-based capital allocation	Implements economic capital allocation and risk adjustment for performance measurement (see Parts 2 and 3 of this text)
Key risk articulation	Is able to name the top risks of the bank at any given time
Risk reporting	Is able to report risk exposures
Safe haven	Provides a place where any employee can report any risk issues without fear of reprisal

managing earnings. When such pressures succeed, risk management practices often are compromised (management may be prone to take more risk) and internal controls may be sacrificed.

Therefore, it is vital that the ERM committee have a thorough understanding of the risks the bank faces. Operational risks, in particular, are susceptible to a weak system of internal controls. Consequently, to ensure that it is well informed about the bank's risk management practices, the committee should ask for a periodic explanation or update on management's risk management efforts, review regulatory and other risk management reports, meet in executive session with the bank's chief risk officer, and recommend an appropriate risk appetite or level of exposure for the bank.

The bank's CRO should regularly report and identify, for the ERM committee, the greatest risks faced by the institution, the probability of those risks occurring, the frequency with which risks may materialize, the impacts if they do occur, and actions being taken by management to mitigate or manage those risks.

To test the effectiveness of management's enterprise risk management program, the ERM committee should:

- Ask for regular reports on risks faced by the company.
- Question management about how corporate objectives are being mapped against risks.
- Examine the effectiveness of early warning indicators.
- Ensure that remedial actions identified by risk management are actually undertaken.
- Ensure that risk management becomes embedded throughout the bank and its corporate culture.

CONCLUSION

Eterprise risk management is a management function, not an audit function. The role of internal audit in any bank's risk management process depends on the sophistication of the risk management program itself. Banks with fledgling programs will benefit greatly from audit's involvement and leadership. However, as the risk management program evolves, it will eventually surpass the abilities and effective contributions of the internal auditor.

Managers and directors also are becoming aware of the limitations of audit's role within ERM. Specifically, while internal audit views and assesses controls at the process level, risk managers view and manage risk at the business level and across various lines of business.

An effective ERM structure will assist management in realizing the bank's business goals and objectives. Combined with a robust system of meaningful reports and assessment methodologies, ERM will enable all stakeholders to improve internal controls, risk measurement, and risk management practices—and to create more value.

The appropriate ERM structure will improve risk management performance, reduce the allocation of resources once spent in managing crisis, redirect resources to other lines of business, reduce the bank's losses and erosion of capital, and increase earnings. In short, a well-conceived ERM structure will minimize surprises and maximize opportunities.

The size and complexity of the bank will dictate the scale of the risk management function. While some banks may employ a few risk analysts, other institutions will employ a substantial number of auditors, analysts, modelers, and managers, all under the direction of a "risk czar," the chief risk officer.

Finally, banks that successfully implement a fully integrated risk management program will be more profitable and resilient than their peers. They will compete more effectively in the market and create tangible value for their stakeholders.

Key Points
Infrastructure to Maximize ERM

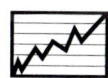

- Every employee of the bank is a risk manager in that every employee must thoughtfully consider risks faced in their business unit every day.
- While the management of risk in terms of "risk silos" is an important first step in developing an acceptable risk management program, ERM considers risks during the strategic-planning process and facilitates the management of risk across departmental products and functions.
- Internal audit, which is integrated into ERM, is a stakeholder in the ERM process.

- The independence of the audit function will not be compromised by reporting to the CRO, as long as the CRO also maintains unrestricted access to the board audit (or ERM) committee.
- For the CRO to succeed in meeting the needs of the board and overcome organizational resistance, he or she must adopt the role of leader, facilitator, negotiator, and ambassador.
- For the risk management program to succeed, risk managers must be independent of the risk-taking functions of the bank.

PART 2
UNDERSTANDING BANK RISKS

To derive more value from the banking and financial services system, bankers now conduct enterprise-wide appraisals of risk factors. Bankers feverishly are trying to assess correlations between previously segregated risk variables so they can better manage these risks throughout their organizations. Estimating these broad-reaching, deeply-penetrating correlations is a challenging exercise—one that, thus far, no one has mastered.

To untangle the correlation riddle, the bank executive first needs to develop and adopt strategies to prepare for, manage, and respond to the individual risk variables. While these variables—credit, market, and, more recently, operational—have long been the focus of bank management, emphasis always has been on their effect on the bottom line: profitability. The goal of ERM, however, is more complex because it aims to reduce earnings volatility, which can then be translated into avoiding losses. In order to support ERM, however, the bank executive needs to analyze, measure, and manage these individual risk variables far beyond the question of profitability.

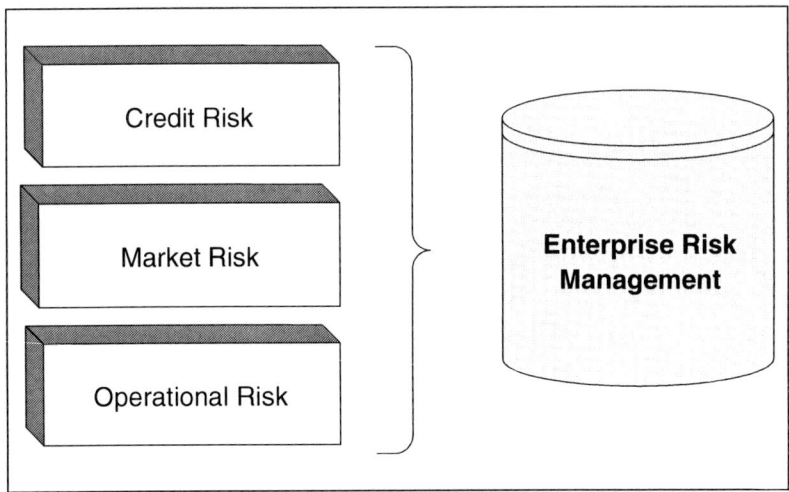

The list of risks to a bank—or any company for that matter—can be endless. In Part 2 of this book, we discuss the three broad categories of risks typically denoted in banks: credit, market, and operational. Each type of risk has a chapter all its own.

Chapter 4
CREDIT RISK

Today the man who is the real risk-taker is anonymous and non-heroic. He is the one trying to make institutions work.
      John William Ward (1922–1985), Princeton University professor

LIED (Loss in the Event of Default) is a phrase frequently used in measuring and monitoring credit risk. We have often wondered if the acronym "LIED" came about because it represented what lenders did when asked to comment on the asset quality of the transaction.

Not that we question the sincerity of lenders (some of the contributors of this book actually are or used to be lenders), but it is no wonder that the Federal Reserve Bank adopted the use of LGD (Loss Given Default) to refer to the same thing. In this case, a rose could not possibly smell as sweet if it were named a thistle or skunk cabbage.

Formula for Success

Credit risk accounts for the vast majority of the risk in the bank's business. A bank executive will be successful if, in a consistent fashion, he or she:

- ► views credit risk in terms of a set of variables—default probability and expected loss
- ► concentrates on deriving the probability of default for the borrower and the severity of potential loss given the actual loan facility

➤ considers possible correlations within the portfolio that may aggravate the bank's risk profile

In this chapter, the bank executive should gain an understanding of the components of credit risk and how to calculate and properly communicate them in the credit portfolio to interested stakeholders.

CREDIT RISK AND PRICING

Credit risk research is a game of Scrabble™ that has lost a few vowels and almost all of its consonants. It comprises a bunch of acronyms ending in D (PD, LGD, EAD, LIED) tangled up with more acronyms ending with an L (EL, UL). So what do all these letters mean to the bank executive? Risk. The D stands for default, the L for loss.

Bankers have always priced transactions to compensate for the risk being underwritten. For as long as bankers have been able to distinguish the risks associated with borrowers, they have charged higher rates and fees to borrowers who appear less likely to make scheduled interest and principal payments and, therefore, are more likely to default.

COMPONENTS OF CREDIT RISK

While post-default restructurings may make secured lenders whole, it is often costly and time consuming. Successful bankers either make "anti-default" bets through hedges or price appropriately for potential defaults.

Consequently, the science of default prediction, explicitly or implicitly, consumes not only bankers but also regulators. Regulators are fascinated by default behavior because defaults add instability to our financial markets. Effectively understanding, predicting, and measuring default is the heart of the current regulatory push to get bankers to adopt adequate practices to assess:

- ▶ Probability of Default
- ▶ Loss Given Default
- ▶ Exposure at Default

Probability of Default

Probability of default (PD) represents the creditworthiness, or riskiness, of a company. The risk grades used in banks are rough predictors of default. The internal-risk grading system, though varying from bank to bank, is straightforward: the better the grade, the better the loan quality and the payback rate. Thus, a better loan grade should have a lower probability of default.

Rating agencies (for example, Fitch, Moody's, and Standard & Poor's) track the rating transition experience, to the point of default, for the entities they rate. This aggregated and published information reflects the migration of ratings from one rating grade to other grades. Of particular interest are those tables showing observed default rates per rating, per year, per industry, per region. For the rated universe, this information reveals the empirical average of the default frequency of companies in each rating category, and it is available in either an average or cumulative basis. As seen in the Average 1-Year Default Rate and the Cumulative 5-Year Default Rate columns (exhibit 4.1) below,[24] better-rated names demonstrate lower default rates.

To date, many middle market companies (the bread and butter lending opportunities for regional and community banks) have not obtained credit ratings for a host of reasons, including that ratings are not necessary for these smaller companies to access capital and also because many cannot afford

Exhibit 4.1 Default Rate (United States 1981–2004)

S&P Rating	Average 1-Year Default Rate (%)	Cumulative 5 Year Default Rate (%)
AAA	0	0
AA	0.01	0.28
A	0.05	0.68
BBB	0.28	2.67
BB	1.14	10.66
B	5.61	25.24
CCC/C	28.42	52.38

the cost of obtaining one. The good news for regional or community banks, however, is that nearly all banks have adopted an internal rating system to rate potential borrowers during the credit approval process. What some bankers do not realize is that these ratings go hand and hand with PD ratings; they become a means by which to "bucket" (categorize) risk.

Rating agencies bucket risk over time in order to label a credit with a rating that will hold "through the cycle" (as opposed to providing a rating that is relevant only when it is issued). As expected, these "through the cycle" ratings are more stable over time. Not all ratings, however, mean the same thing. An S&P rating reflects the likelihood of default (probability of default). A Moody's rating, in contrast, is an opinion on expected loss (a product of the probability of default as well as loss severity). Unfortunately, to date, rating agencies only track companies until default, so there is no easy way to tap into a central data repository that tracks credit statistics of companies through the default and recovery process.

While the rating agencies and other data vendors provide useful information to guide bank executives, the most likely course of action for regional and community bankers is to first examine their own data to classify meaningful default probabilities for their borrowers (discussed below). Additionally, bank executives may want to reach out to their peer banks to share data. This undertaking, however, requires that the sharing institutions apply similar definitions of default (for instance, default may be recorded when interest or principal payments are past due 90 days, or in some other fashion).

Loss Given Default

Loss given default, or LGD, refers to the fraction of the total exposure that the bank expects to lose on each defaulted asset. The degree of loss reflects both the macroeconomic environment as well as the traits of the loan facility. In other words, the amount of loss the bank will experience, given a default, depends not only on the timing of the default, but also on the loan's structural characteristics (that is, lien position, debt cushion, and nature of collateral). LGD is equivalent to 1 minus the recovery rate; thus, the recovery rate is the percentage of the loan amount that can be recovered. (See chapter 7 for calculations.)

Exposure at Default

When a default occurs, any amount left outstanding on the loan is the exposure at default, or EAD. The Basel II definition of EAD consists of two parts: the amount currently drawn on a credit, and an estimate of future draw-downs of available but untapped credit. EAD, therefore, applies to nonterm exposures only, such as unfunded loan commitments and lines of credit. Depending on the structure of a loan transaction, a borrower may not be able to draw against the available line once the credit is in default.

DUAL RATING SCALES

Many banks in the United States are upgrading their traditional, internal one-dimensional rating scales to more sophisticated matrix approaches. Historically, banks have used single-dimension scales to address creditworthiness of borrowers as well as facility features such as collateral quality. However, banking is more of a science than an art. Increasingly, banks are finding value in systems that differentiate the borrower's characteristics from those of the facility (or loan), which is the LGD amount discussed above.

It is important to stress that while the PD is for the borrowing entity/obligor, LGD refers back to the loan facility. Various loans to a single borrower may be secured by different collateral, or the loan facility type may vary from loan to loan. For example, a particular borrower conducts business in such a way as to garner a single likelihood of default. That borrower, however, may require multiple loans: one to build an apartment complex and another to provide working capital for a construction business. The risk of each loan may be different because, although the loans are to the same borrower, the collateral packages differ. An apartment complex secures the construction loan, whereas liquid assets secure the working capital loan. This differentiation can be better identified by a dual-rating scale than by a single-dimension system. The borrower has a single PD, whereas the two different facilities represent two different LGDs.

EXPECTED LOSS

Expected loss (EL) is the level of loss to which a bank is exposed on average over the loan term. Typically, EL is addressed when pricing is set and reserves are established against expected losses (whereas capital charges are set to cover unexpected losses). Referring back to the three components of credit risk (PD, LGD, and EAD), expected loss is easy to calculate. The product of these measures (more on the actual calculations in chapter 7) is visually represented in the expected loss matrix (exhibit 4.2).

The range of probabilities of default (PDs) for the loans in the banking book runs down the vertical axis. These PDs may be based on either historic values (for example, what is the percentage of loans that defaulted in each loan grade in previous years?) or projected values (for example, what does management believe the percentage of default in each grade will be?), depending on the analysis being performed and the availability of data. The range of loss given default (LGD) is along the horizontal axis. Although this range also may be based on historical data, it is more likely to be based on projections. The diagonal line through the matrix represents the expected loss levels that are a product of the PD and LGD ranges. The top

EXHIBIT 4.2 Expected Loss Matrix

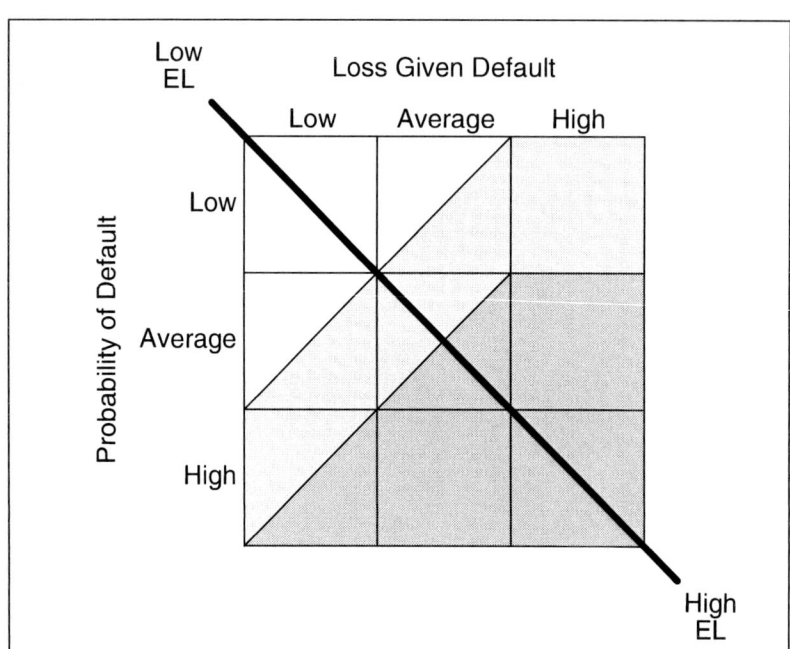

left, lighter region (low expected loss) represents high-quality loans with low PD and low LGD, and the bottom right darkly-shaded area (high expected loss) contains loans likely to default with low recovery value.

Insights

Understanding the definitions of default and loss is easy. Capturing and maintaining a relevant data set is the challenge. Fitting inhouse data into this simple diagram helps establish the dimensions of risk measurement.

Risk measurement is a two-part exercise. The first step is to understand the bank's tolerance of expected loss in terms of PD and LGD by sketching its internal risk-rating system into the matrix. The second step is to overlay the bank's historical data onto the matrix to see how actual lending experiences have played out and to determine if the institution actually has been rewarded for the risk it has underwritten.

To fit the bank's existing internal rating scale into the matrix, first overlay the internal-rating scale along the "probability of default" axis of a blank matrix. Which ratings do you consider to have a "low" PD versus an "average" versus a "high"? Then, apply values to the "loss given default" axis based either on expectations or actual loss history.

To see how the bank's lending history played out on the expected loss line, plot the bank's lending experiences against this matrix. How many experiences have there been of a loan with a "low" PD experiencing a "low" LGD? How many with an "average" LGD, and how many with a "high"? Complete this exercise for all historical data available, and the resulting scatter diagram will provide a visualization of how the bank's historical lending record played out on the expected loss scale. Finally, to provide perspective on how well the bank has been compensated for the risk it has underwritten, overlay the pricing associated with the data points on the expected loss matrix. How does this picture fit with the risk profile that bank management has set strategically?

The bank executive may want to add another dimension to this analysis: the quantity of loans at each PD/LGD combination. The resulting array of clusters provides insights into the value of lending to borrowers with certain characteristics, such as types of collateral. This exercise can be conducted at the portfolio level or by book of business or some other subsection, such as by lending group.

Given certain asset classes, one might expect to see certain patterns. For instance, based on their secured nature and the quality of their underlying collateral, ABL (asset based lending) loans should have lower LGD than broader cash-flow lending. Leveraged buyouts (LBOs) may have medium-high PDs because of their high leverage and strong cash flow, but low to medium LGD because of the security package that is likely to include all assets or all current assets.

Clearly, loans migrate over time, from better rating grades to lower rating grades. This migration is most likely tracked by the bank's portfolio management group. The value in using this matrix is that it helps explain loan migration in a systematic fashion. The goal of managing the portfolio is to be compensated for EL. This matrix helps the bank executive monitor the portfolio in an effort to avoid traveling down the dark diagonal line. Bankers understand that it is difficult to maintain a loan portfolio with stable default rates, but striving to meet collateral and covenant quality standards will limit LGD travel in the wrong direction across the recovery horizon.

Acceptable Risks

At this point, the bank executive probably has a strong sense of what expected loss is acceptable. The matrix is a tool to enable lenders in the organization to visualize the potential combinations of PD and LGD that are acceptable to the portfolio management team. Shading the matrix highlights different risk levels, such as those that are desirable, less desirable, or unpalatable. The matrix also emphasizes how risk results equally from the PD as well as LGD halves of the whole. A credit with a high PD but low LGD is equally as costly as another with a low PD but high LGD.

For instance, in exhibit 4.2 the unshaded area represents where loans quickly can be approved (the challenge here will be to earn a sufficient return), the lightly shaded area will likely represent many of your lending opportunities, and the "dark side" reflects unattractive deals based on your bank's risk profile. Of course, these lending/portfolio decisions need to be viewed in conjunction with required return parameters at your bank.

This matrix can be a guideline understood throughout the bank for originators, portfolio managers, and credit administration. As facilities make the transition to a lower rating grade, they will move from an acceptable EL level to a less desirable one. Such facilities may require more monitoring or may no longer meet portfolio standards, and action should be taken to remove them from the portfolio.

To make this picture more granular, the matrix is converted into a table with numbers reflecting an example bank's internal rating system and associated PDs, as well as numbers reflecting LGD (exhibit 4.3). The terms describing asset quality reflect the recovery (1 − LGD) potential. The product of these numbers, PDs and LGDs, equal ELs and are shown in the cells of the exhibit

A borrower who is classified a risk grade of 9 with a high recovery rate (expect to recover 90 percent) has an EL of 2.5 percent. Perhaps this is undesirable to your financial institution. Exhibit 4.3 shows that a borrower with a risk grade of 6 and no chance of recovery also has an EL of 2.5 percent. What is the likelihood that credits in the bank's portfolio have migrated

EXHIBIT 4.3 Expected Loss (Illustrative)

Risk Grade: Obligor Rating–Average PD	Obligor Rating	Average 5 Year PD	Asset Quality: Loss Given Default			
			High ≤10%	Good 11 to 30%	Adequate 31 to 60%	Poor 61 to 100%
	1	0.04%	0.00%	0.01%	0.02%	0.04%
	2	0.10%	0.01%	0.03%	0.06%	0.10%
	3	0.30%	0.03%	0.09%	0.18%	0.30%
	4	0.80%	0.08%	0.24%	0.48%	0.80%
	5	1.50%	0.15%	0.45%	0.90%	1.50%
	6	2.50%	0.25%	0.75%	1.50%	2.50%
	7	4.00%	0.40%	1.20%	2.40%	4.00%
	8	10.00%	1.00%	3.00%	6.00%	10.00%
	9	25.00%	2.50%	7.50%	15.00%	25.00%
	10	50.00%	5.00%	15.00%	30.00%	50.00%

down to a grade 6 during the past few years? Is the bank executive consistently considering, either by quantitatively estimating and/or qualitatively assessing, the recovery prospects for these loans? Has the bank examined the possibility that these two expected loss scenarios are being managed differently? There may be a good reason for setting different criteria for the loan portfolio, depending on risk grades, recovery potential, and so forth. Using this EL matrix may help to further refine the bank's approach.

In addition to stating that certain return thresholds must be met, using a matrix like this can help originators, portfolio managers, and credit officers understand tolerance levels for the components of expected loss. This tool communicates a clear preference for doing business with more or less risky customers, depending on the asset quality of their businesses. Plus, as facilities make the transition to a lower rating grade, they are likely to move from an acceptable to a less desirable EL level.

Management Expectations

By comparing borrowers on this matrix, bankers can determine if the portfolio is in line with management strategy and expectations. Plus, this summary picture can make visualizing the effects of a triggering event an easier exercise on various sectors of the portfolio: for instance a war, the landfall of a major hurricane, a 20 percent hike in oil prices, and so forth.

Effectively, this table splits expected loss into its two dimensions: default and loss. To incorporate tolerance for EAD, the bank executive can introduce exposure levels into the picture.

An additional and useful exercise for bank executives is to explore further the drivers for default and loss at the bank. The default and loss axes can be differentiated further by identifying/listing traits explaining why borrowers default on loans, as well as characteristics (for example, secured versus unsecured, loans to particular industries, collateralized by property in certain geographical regions, and so forth) leading to various loss levels. This exercise requires a banker to analyze all defaults and recoveries to date, in which the bank executive examines similar loan characteristics that tend to lead to default and to collection trends. This analysis should be done with a team of senior lenders and credit staff who create and review a list of characteristics linked to default and recovery experience. If the bank has not already explored this analysis, the bank executive may wish to examine work done by the rating agencies. Standard &Poor's, for example, provides consulting to help banks analyze/categorize their loss and recovery history by loan characteristics. CreditPro™, an S&P tool, contains S&P's ratings history and allows the user to cut the data by sector, issuance year, rating, and so forth.

Evaluating the bank's expected loss matrix will prove valuable to management making capital allocation, lending, and pricing decisions. This depiction of the expected loss matrix will be useful when communicating with the board, employees, stakeholders, and regulators.[25]

CONCLUSION

Regardless of your bank's intentions with respect to Basel II, paying attention to the components of credit risk supported by sound practices in data collection, maintenance, and analysis is important for any well-managed bank. The business of managing data can take on a life of its own. Being grounded with the ultimate goal of best managing enterprise risk is the starting point. Estimating capital/reserves needed to optimize credit risk (that is, balancing risk with reward) requires having clear objectives before undertaking any data capture or manipulation.

Key Points
Credit Risk

- Three basic components are used to determine credit risk: probability of default (PD), loss given default (LGD), and exposure at default (EAD).
- A simple expected loss matrix is used to visualize the riskiness of a particular credit.
- Examine what matters: What is driving default and, ultimately, loss? Remember that the goal of this exercise is to help you manage credit risk better.

Chapter 5
MARKET RISK

The man who knows it can't be done counts the risk, not the reward.
Elbert Hubbard (1856–1915), U.S. author

The Economist magazine uses something called the "Big Mac Index" to determine purchasing power parity across various countries. Why McDonald's Big Mac? That particular burger is sold in over 100 countries with nearly the same recipe in each.

So what does the Big Mac tell us about market risk? Purchasing power parity theory states that over time, if exchange rates are behaving as they should, an identical basket of goods would cost the same in any country. The Big Mac is one of the few items that would qualify in an identical basket of goods. Consequently, it is an excellent measure of the risk in currency exchange rates, determining whether a currency is valued properly. If a Big Mac costs $2.29 in Wichita, it should cost $2.29 in Beijing. The variance between the two in U.S dollars is a measure of the market risk inherent in exchange rates. And if a Big Mac fails to suit your taste, you can always try the Starbucks Tall Latte Index.

Formula for Success
In truly understanding bank risks, the bank executive should know the types of risks that comprise market risk and how it is measured. The bank executive will be successful if he or she does the following:

- views market risk as the "mature" risk; that is, sees it as a risk that has been studied and modeled for a long time
- understands the two types of market risk that concern community banks most
- uses value-at-risk measures to understand and communicate market risks to management

This chapter covers the two main market risks most community banks encounter: interest rate risk and liquidity risk. It also explains the traditional method (VAR) used to measure market risk.

A Perspective

In previous decades, financial intermediaries operated with one risk in mind: credit risk. That rather simple business strategy of paying interest on deposits while lending those funds at a higher rate has had much proven success. Protecting the bank's assets from credit risk—the risk that a borrower fails to pay his obligations—remains a basic task for the bank executive.

Whereas credit risk is fairly straightforward, there are many different types of market risks. They differ from industry to industry, from bank to bank. Currency risk plays a key role in managing an international bank, whereas a community bank's exposure to it is limited. Banks that specialize in complex financial instrument structures expose themselves to excessive management costs and losses.[26]

The Mature Risk

Market risk arises from unexpected movements in market prices or rates. Although considered separate from two other broad risk types (credit and operational), market risk is closely aligned with them. Operational losses at European and North American financial institutions have caused not only financial losses, but also a decline in market value.[27] Huge credit defaults will lead to interest rate changes and, therefore, to market loss.[28]

Market risk is the most mature of the three risk management disciplines (credit, market, and operational). Market risk management practices, on the other hand, vary from a very basic degree where a bank evaluates the impact of market risk factors on earnings to a more advanced, best practice level, where managing market risk moves from a corporate control function to a money-making proposition.[29] The best-practices bank views market risk as both potential for adverse consequences and as opportunity for increased earnings.

Market risk is managed when bank executives set tolerances for exposures defined in value-at-risk (VAR) measures and independently monitor them.[30] There are two types of market risk—interest rate and liquidity—on which community banks are most focused (see exhibit 5.1).

Interest-Rate Risk

Simply the natural progression of managing credit risks, interest-rate-risk management became a part of good bank management long before the regulatory entities made it a priority. Interest-rate risk is the "potential variability in a bank's net interest income and the market value of equity due to changes in the level of market interest rates."[31] It causes the bank executive to monitor the changes in interest rates to improve interest-rate risk management.

It is possible to add value to a bank by managing the level of interest-rate risk despite the difficulty in forecasting interest rates.[32]

EXHIBIT 5.1 Market Risk

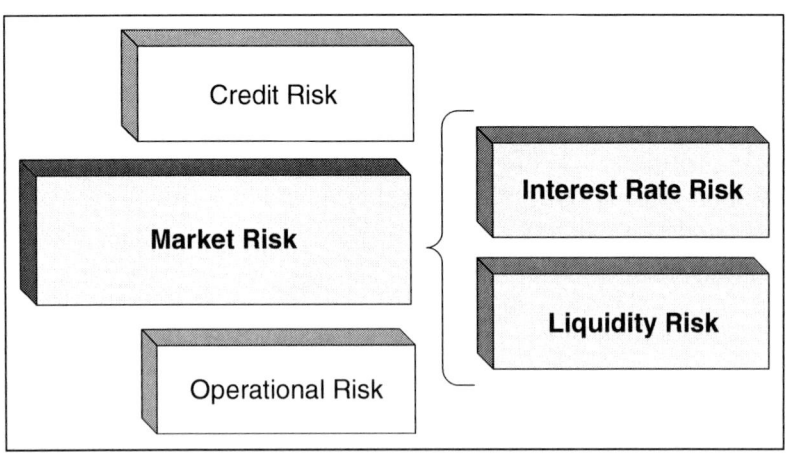

Liquidity Risk

Choosing to ignore more sophisticated methodology in measuring and managing all risks can cause an adverse rating or grade change from ratings agencies or regulators, which affects a bank's ability to obtain funds from an outside source at reasonable cost (chapter 1). This circumstance is at the heart of liquidity risk.

The traditional view of liquidity risk correlates directly to a bank's quick ratio. That is, the relationship of current assets to current liabilities determines liquidity: how long does it take to convert an asset to cash? However, viewing liquidity risk in this simplistic way diminishes the bank executive's ability to foresee unexpected loss.

Another perspective (and a better one) on viewing liquidity risk is gained by determining a bank's financial flexibility—its ability to supplement future cash flows to cover any unexpected needs or to take advantage of unexpected opportunities. In managing liquidity risk properly, a bank executive must consider the bank's earnings stability, its debt-to-equity position, the secondary marketability of investments, and the availability of credit lines.[33]

It is generally believed that the best way to measure expected and unexpected loss in the market is through value-at-risk (VAR) methodology. Though originally it was intended for use within securities firms and investments banks, commercial banks and other financial institutions also adopted VAR and extended its use to measuring credit and liquidity risks. There are problems with VAR, as we shall see later in the chapter, but a basic understanding of VAR is essential not only in critically thinking about risks,[34] but also in communicating the risks posed to the bank.

VALUE-AT-RISK

If the reader is already familiar with VAR, he or she may skip to the next section on bank market risks without any loss of

EXHIBIT 5.2 Periodic Return on Investment Fund

Period	Periodic Return	Change in Yield from the Prior Period
1	80.7	3.46%
2	82.3	2.02%
3	81.1	−1.50%
4	81.0	−0.12%
5	82.0	1.23%
6	83.9	2.32%
7	86.4	3.01%
8	86.6	0.20%
9	84.2	−2.77%
10	83.8	−0.48%
11	83.3	−0.60%
12	88.3	6.00%
13	93.8	6.23%
14	94.4	0.64%
15	96.3	2.01%
16	95.7	−0.62%
17	96.3	0.63%
18	97.3	1.04%
19	101.1	3.91%
20	104.4	3.26%
21	103.2	−1.15%
22	102.0	−1.16%
23	98.5	−3.43%
24	99.0	0.51%
25	100.1	1.11%
26	97.6	−2.50%
27	98.6	1.02%
28	100.8	2.23%
29	104.8	3.97%
30	102.9	−1.80%

continuity. The rest of this section includes a basic discussion about VAR.

Consider a $10,000 noninsured investment into a fund whose historic returns are depicted in exhibit 5.2. The change in its annual returns appears in exhibit 5.3. This fund contains both negative and positive returns, illustrating that the value of the investment is at risk: it can lose money.

The next step in calculating VAR is to determine the interval of the return and to distribute the returns within those intervals. In our example, the fund gained almost 7 percent in one year and lost nearly 4 percent in another. Each interval, then, is one percentage point (that is, 7% to 6%, 6% to 5%, 5% to 4%, and so forth). The number of returns or observations that fall within each interval is shown in exhibit 5.4 and illustrated in exhibit 5.5.

Next, determine the probability of each return, selecting a confidence level of, say, 90 percent; that is, finding a loss that will occur 10 percent of the time only (or will not occur 90 percent of the time). The example of 30 points of return data means that 3 (30 times 10 percent) observations will be lower than the stated confidence level, as in exhibit 5.6.

EXHIBIT 5.3 Change in Periodic Return

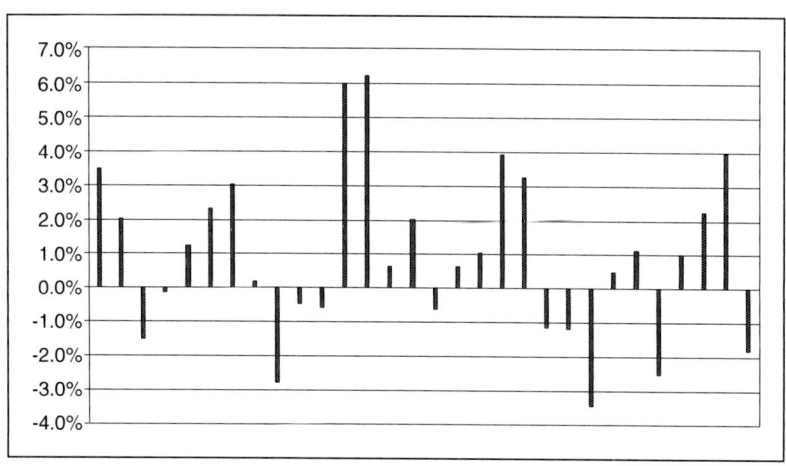

EXHIBIT 5.4 Number of Occurrences

Change in Return Interval		
Between	**and**	**Number of Occurrences in Data**
7%	6%	2
6%	5%	0
5%	4%	0
4%	3%	5
3%	2%	4
2%	1%	4
1%	0%	4
0%	−1%	4
−1%	−2%	4
−2%	−3%	2
−3%	−4%	1

EXHIBIT 5.5 Histogram of Occurrences

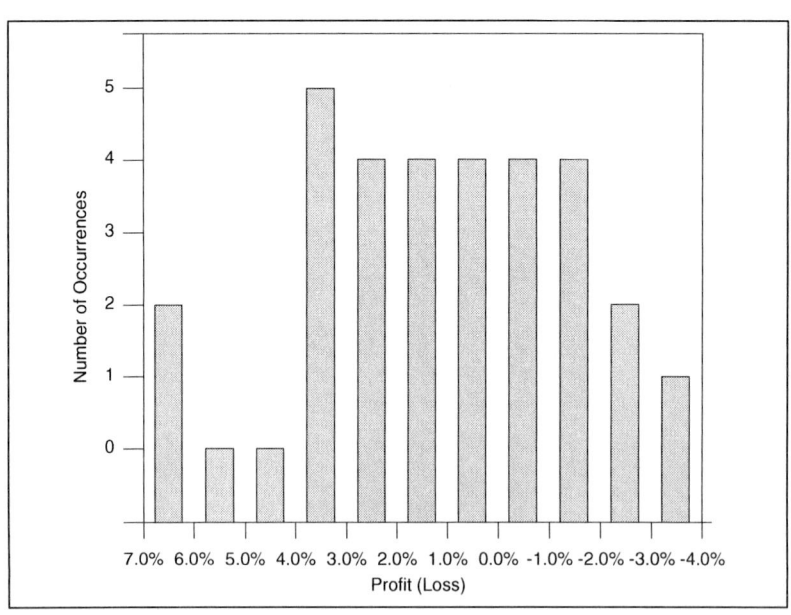

EXHIBIT 5.6 90 Percent Confidence Level

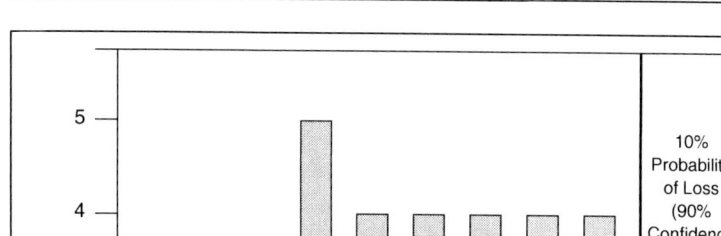

For our $10,000 invested in this fund, this means that at a 90-percent confidence level the most the fund can lose over a one-year period is about –2.2 percent (where the probability of loss hits the histogram data), or $10,000 × –2.2% = –$220. Therefore, the VAR for this investment is $220. For the statistically precise reader, the standard deviation of the returns over the period is 2.42: 90 percent of 2.42 is 2.18, making a precise VAR of $218.

Communicating Value-at-Risk

Communicated to the average banker or director, value-at-risk typically translates to: with 90 percent probability or confidence level, the most this investment can lose over a one-year period is $218 under normal market conditions. Preferable, however, is using natural frequencies[35] in communicating the value-at-risk: *when market conditions are as they are today, in 9 out of 10 years, the most the investment will lose is $218.* In other words, expect an actual loss of $218 or less (it could be $200, or $50, or $1.98). However, this simplistic analysis does not give a probability of any particular loss amount.

What, exactly, is meant by a confidence level? Using probabilities can further muddy already muddied waters.

For instance, what does a 30 percent chance of rain forecast for today mean? Is it that it will rain for 30 percent of the day, or 7.2 of 24 hours? Does it mean that it will rain in 30 percent of the forecast area? Prior to the early 1960s, probabilities were not used in forecasting weather.[36] Rather, meteorologists and "Weather Girls" alike used a much easier-to-understand statement: In three out of every ten days with current conditions, it will rain for some part of the day. That is a big difference from 7.2 hours of rain in a 24-hour period. When calculating the risks of getting wet, it is helpful to know when to carry an umbrella.

Unexpected Loss

VAR gives the bank executive a metric for estimating the loss expected over a given time period and a given confidence level. In other words, VAR indicates the most a bank can expect to lose in the normal course of business and *not* in the event of an unexpected occurrence. In our example, we know that we can expect to lose $218 at most on our $10,000 investment in 9 out of 10 years, but we have no idea how much we can lose in that tenth or bad year.

Taken a step farther, VAR can be compared to the important concept of unexpected loss (UL)[37] measure one needs to calculate risk-based capital. Unexpected loss gives us a metric for determining an estimate of what can be lost beyond the level of confidence; it gives us an idea of how bad things can get (VAR tells us only that there could be a loss higher than the VAR itself).[38]

Going back to our $10,000 example, we can turn our data into a probabilities-of-loss illustration. To derive an unexpected loss metric, calculate nine more confidence levels in the direction of more confidence, along the "tail" of the distribution (at 91%, 92%, 93%, and so forth) and take the average (exhibits 5.7 and 5.8).

Given our $10,000 investment, when market conditions are as they are today, in 9 out of 10 years, the most the investment will lose is $218 (assuming a 90 percent confidence level and a VAR of 2.18). In a bad market, the investment will lose the average of the VARs, $228. Exhibit 5.8 illustrates loss provisions for expected losses, economic capital for unexpected losses, and catastrophic losses. Should something catastrophic occur, it is beyond VAR's capability to adequately measure. A catastrophy is covered neither by expected losses (presumably built into loss provisions and routine operating losses) or unexpected losses (covered by economic capital). Insurance and other risk mitigants come into play here.

EXHIBIT 5.7 Estimating Unexpected Loss as an Average of VARs

Confidence Levels	VAR Values
91%	2.20
92%	2.22
93%	2.25
94%	2.27
95%	2.30
96%	2.32
97%	2.34
98%	2.37
99%	2.39
Average of VARs:	2.28

EXHIBIT 5.8 Expected, Unexpected, and Catastrophic Losses

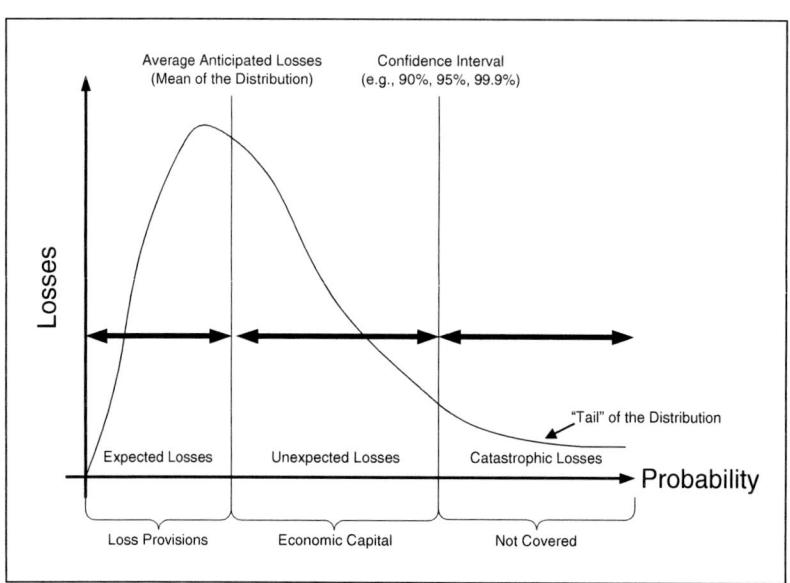

CONCLUSION

Volatile interest rates cause bankers and regulators alike to pay close attention to market risk, specifically interest rate risk and liquidity risk. Though these fundamental market risks are the focus of this chapter, an understanding of value-at-risk (VAR) is important for the discussion of bank market risk.

Though in the "mature" category, market risk cannot take a back seat in enterprise risk management. It is important for the bank executive to stretch beyond traditional views and see market-risk measurement and management for the value-added service it performs.

Key Points
Market Risk

- Market risk, particularly for a community bank, is focused on two types of risk: interest rate and liquidity.
- Interest rate risk is the potential variability in a bank's net interest income and market value of equity due to changes in the level of market interest rates.
- A bank's ability to supplement its future cash flows to cover any unexpected needs or to take advantage of unexpected opportunities plays an important role in determining liquidity risk.
- Value-at-risk (VAR), the traditional measure of risk, can be used to determine expected and unexpected losses in a bank's portfolio.

Chapter 6

OPERATIONAL RISK*

*Proverbial wisdom counsels against risk and change.
But sitting ducks fare worst of all.*
Mason Cooley (b. 1927), U.S. aphorist

The alligator allegory to Murphy's Law is a fitting tribute to operational risk managers: Executives should be able to thoroughly analyze company objectives and anticipate every problem before it occurs. The bank executive then has to have answers to each anticipated problem and solve them the moment they arise. Unfortunately, when you are up to your neck in alligators, one forgets that the first objective is to drain the swamp.

Formula for Success

Operational risk is somewhat of a "catch-all" category in the world of risk management. Each bank has its own unique set of operational risks that create a labyrinth of complexities for a bank executive. To manage operational risk successfully, a bank executive should:

- ▶ recognize that operational risk is not limited to the IT area of the bank
- ▶ recognize that operational risk exists in any transaction, process, or system—automated or manual

---

*Ali Samad-Khan is the principal author of this chapter.

- identify, assess, and evaluate past operational losses
- manage current risks to the operation in addition to market and credit risks

---

This chapter covers the fundamentals of operational risk, including its definition and ways to evaluate it. It also discusses some low-tech, inexpensive, and quick-to-implement tools with which to assess operational risks.

MODERN OPERATIONAL RISK

With a Basel II focus on operational risk, it appears that banks have discovered something new. But operational risk is not new. Most successful firms have been effectively managing operational risk since they began. But as organizations strive to remain competitive in today's complex global economy, they are exposed to new forms of risk. Managing a twenty-first century portfolio of risks can be daunting, as evidenced by the staggering amounts of money numerous firms have lost as a result of operational failures.

FUNDAMENTALS OF OPERATIONAL RISK MANAGEMENT

As the world changes, organizations are discovering that effective operational risk management goes beyond simply building "awareness" among staff in the hope that sound risk management practices will emerge spontaneously. Pragmatists know that effectively managing operational risk involves creating the right culture, a culture designed to turn awareness into action. But getting managers to act optimally requires the right set of incentives, because people do what they have an incentive to do and generally avoid those things with little to no incentive.

Effective operational risk management requires a significant effort. First, an organization must identify and assess its real risks accurately. Second, these risks must be assigned to their natural business "owners." (These are the people who have a natural interest in mitigating the identified risks and the ability to effect change.) Third, there must be a method for objectively measuring the quality of the internal controls corresponding to each risk. Fourth, there needs to be a transparent process for monitoring changes in the level of risks and their corresponding controls, both of which must be gauged against a set of tolerance standards. Finally, there must be an equitable process—with clear and unambiguous financial incentives—to ensure that the right risks are being mitigated efficiently and in the context of a cost-benefit analysis.

Many organizations aspire to this level of excellence, but few manage to achieve it. Sound operational risk management begins with a comprehensive understanding of certain fundamental concepts, many of which are not well understood. In this chapter, we examine some of these core concepts.

Operational Risk Defined

Operational risk is defined as "the risk of loss resulting from inadequate or failed internal processes, people and systems, or from external events."[39] In contrast to market risk, there is generally no upside potential in operational risk.[40] Rather, operational risk management is about mitigating or avoiding risk. Thus, operational risk is measured in terms of the magnitude of loss potential at a specified level of uncertainty.

Some think of operational risk in the context of a single event, for example, the risk of having a fire. But because it is possible for an organization to experience more than one fire per year, practitioners view operational risk as not just the uncertainty associated with a single fire loss, but instead as the uncertainty associated with multiple fire losses. Fundamentally, operational risk management is about mitigating the risk of the full spectrum of operational losses. It is not possible to know, for example, whether the risk of fires is greater than the risk of transaction process errors without understanding whether the cumulative risk of fire losses (the total amount of money an organization could lose from all fires experienced in one year) is greater that the cumulative risk of transaction processing error losses (the total amount of money the firm could lose from all transaction processing errors experienced in one year).

Expected and Unexpected Operational Loss

While the terms "expected loss" and "unexpected loss" are ubiquitous in the risk management industry, much confusion exists about what they really mean. They make sense only in the context of statistical analysis. For example, under the Value-at-Risk (VAR) approach discussed in chapter 5, these terms describe features of a loss distribution (see exhibit 5.8). In operational risk management, because the concern is with the cumulative or total amount of money that could be lost during one time period, aggregate loss potential is analyzed. An aggregate loss distribution, which factors in both the number of losses (frequency) and the magnitude of loss (severity), maps probabilities against aggregate loss exposure.

Because the expected loss is the amount of money a business loses on average in one year, it is also the amount a business should budget to cover its annual operational failure cost. The unexpected loss is the amount a bank could lose in a very bad year in excess of the budgeted amount, and it is the amount the bank ought to reserve as capital. As with market risk, most risk management industry professionals view the unexpected loss, expressed in VAR terms, as the most accurate representation of risk.

Inherent Risk

Some think of inherent risk as the type or level of risk before controls. But this definition leads to confusion because risk without controls may be infinite. Consider a practical example. If one has a million dollars in a safe and leaves it unguarded and wide open (no controls), what is the likely range of outcomes? He or she would probably lose every penny. The "risk" would appear to be exactly one million dollars—which is equivalent to the maximum exposure.[41] Since the concept of inherent risk is meant to convey something different from maximum exposure, it is clear that "risk without controls" is not an appropriate way of describing inherent risk.

A more practical definition of inherent risk may be the level of risk associated with an optimal control environment, where the controls are no greater nor any less than those required for optimum economic profit. With this definition, the bank executive could then use different aggregate loss distributions to show the inherent differences in the risk profiles of different businesses (see exhibit 6.1). It is also much easier to explain inherent risk in terms of two variables, such as expected and unexpected loss, because in many cases the VAR-to-mean ratio highlights the inherent differences in the risk profiles among businesses and risk types.

TYPES OF OPERATIONAL RISKS

Hundreds of different types of operational risks confront banks. The lists of operational risks developed in every company

EXHIBIT 6.1 Risk Profiles of Two Different Lines of Business

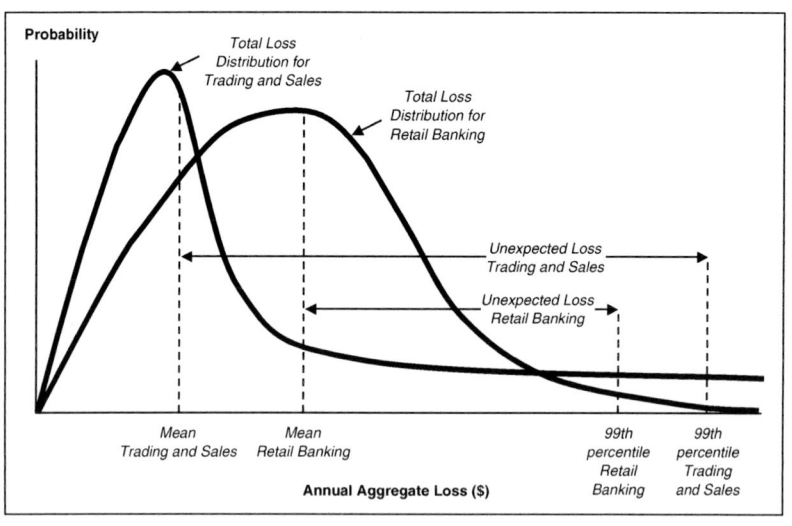

depend on a variety of things, such as industry, geographical area, business model, size, management style, and so forth. In this book, operational risks are discussed as a spectrum of risks and include a broader discussion on four major risks that banks—and most companies—experience: legal risk, reputation risk, regulatory risk, and strategic risk (see exhibit 6.2). The discussion on these four risks, therefore, should not be considered the conclusive word on operational risk but, rather, an illustrative one. The implementation tools explained later in this chapter will be illustrated using these four major operational risks.

Legal Risk

As with any business in the modern economy, legal risk is inherent in almost every facet of the banking operation. It

EXHIBIT 6.2 Types of Operational Risk

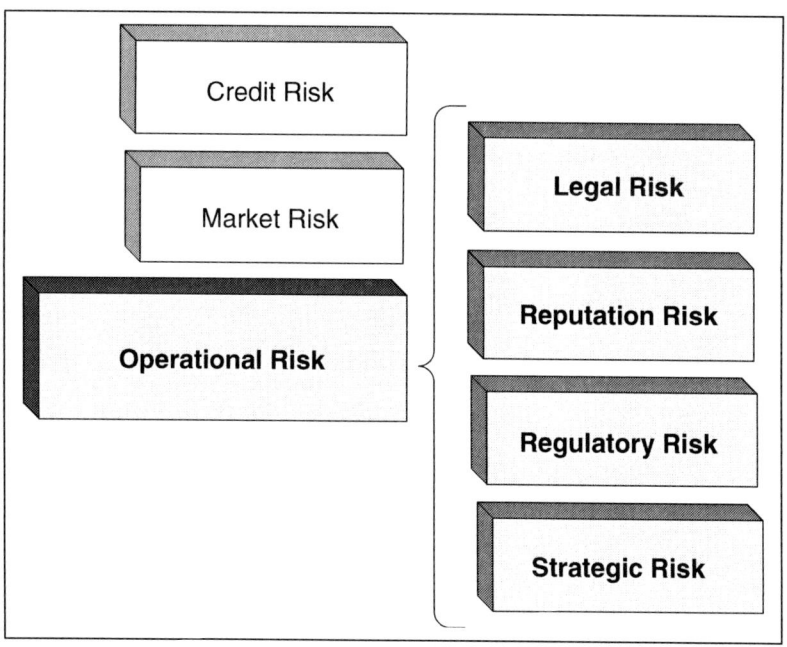

includes "the potential that unenforceable contracts, lawsuits, or adverse judgments can disrupt or otherwise negatively affect the operations or condition of a banking organization."[42]

Eliminating risks is not the risk officer's goal; his or her goal is to identify and manage risks effectively and to be compensated for assuming them. When considering legal risk, the risk officer's first level of inquiry is to identify how legal risk manifests itself within the commercial banking organization. This is especially important in the context of identifying who is responsible for managing that risk. For instance, the legal risk associated with an unenforceable promissory note for a consumer loan most likely resides in the loan operations group. If this function is responsible for document production and file maintenance, the people in that function are best suited to manage the process of document and information control, in an effort to mitigate this risk. Similarly, legal risk associated with employment relationships, such as wrongful termination, harassment, discrimination, wage and hour disputes, and so forth, may reside in the human resources or training groups. While it is often tempting to assign responsibility for legal risks to the compliance or legal departments, a well-functioning, effective risk management program will not accede to this simplistic approach.

Identifying and Measuring Legal Risk. It is essential to identify and measure the specific inherent legal risks within each facet of the banking business. Unenforceable contracts, for example, contain multiple specific risks. Perhaps the simplest example of risk relating to unenforceable contracts would be flaws in a promissory note or security agreement that would impede the bank in its collection efforts against a defaulted borrower. Another example would be flaws in account documentation that may limit the bank's remedies against the customer, such as a flawed set-off provision in a deposit agreement. As to contract disputes, legal risk may arise because of a dissatisfied counter-party in a contract situation, or flawed or vague language contained in an agreement.

An effective risk management program will identify the universe of contracts in the organization, place them into manageable, well-defined categories, and assign a level of legal risk inherent in each category (such as "Vendor Contracts," "Treasury Instruments," "Leases," and the like). The degree of commonality of the contracts within the category should drive the level of specificity of the categories.

The quantification of inherent risk associated with each category should be a function of both the likelihood of noncompliance with its terms and the scope, scale, or impact of the consequence of noncompliance as discussed earlier.

Although lawsuits are not a part of a business process per se, they are a derivative of all business processes in a commercial bank. Lawsuits have the potential to affect asset values, litigation expense, internal resources (time and attention), the reputation of the franchise, and of course, fines and penalties. Perhaps the most challenging part of an effective legal risk management program is the measurement of legal risks. Legal risks are, by their very nature, difficult to quantify and often must be evaluated on a "what if" or "worst-case" basis. A simple and practical place to start in evaluating legal risk is to review the bank's annual audit inquiry letters.

Mitigation of Legal Risks. Once a bank executive has identified and measured legal risk on a consistent basis, the next step is to develop a program to monitor and mitigate that risk. Generally, the regulatory agencies measure the adequacy of a legal risk management program by assessing the banking organization's (1) policies, procedures, and risk limits; (2) board and management oversight; (3) systems of internal controls; and (4) day-to-day risk monitoring practices.[43]

Risk monitoring practices are undoubtedly the most important components of an effective legal risk management program, and awareness of the risks associated with each aspect of the business is essential for effective monitoring. This emphasizes the need for comprehensive training of personnel at all levels of the organization and for procedures for keeping abreast of legal and regulatory developments. In the wake of the Sarbanes–Oxley Act and revisions to the U.S. Sentencing Guidelines, the level of employee awareness and participation in compliance programs, the tone at the top, ethics, and a culture of compliance with laws and regulations have had a direct and significant bearing on the level of legal and regulatory risk assumed by an institution. It is also essential that an institution involve legal counsel in developing new products, expanding into new jurisdictions, and contracting with third parties.

Another aspect of mitigating legal risk includes using tools such as insurance or reserves to limit the financial exposure to risk. An effective legal risk-mitigation program will periodically assess the sufficiency of insurance coverage relative to the size, complexity, and risk profile of the institution. Variables in insurance coverage include coverage limits, retention levels, and coverage terms and conditions. Even though contingency reserves most often are considered in the context of litigation, they may be appropriate in a broader sense when entering into a new line of business, expanding into a new jurisdiction, or contracting with a new third party.

Summary of Legal Risks. Legal risk resides in almost every facet of the commercial banking organization. An effective risk management program ensures that the responsibility for managing legal risk resides at the line level. But to do so requires a commitment to training and awareness programs, as well as a consistent methodology to identify and measure legal risk so that it may be effectively prioritized and mitigated by modifying processes, reallocating risk, establishing reserves, or insuring the risk.

Reputation Risk

> *It takes twenty years to build a reputation
> and five minutes to ruin it.*
> Warren Buffett, Chairman and CEO, Berkshire Hathaway

If you read, watch the news, or shop, odds are you realize that reputation matters. Over the past thirty years, business leaders have recognized the necessity of building and sustaining a favorable corporate reputation to develop strategy and to create competitive advantage. A favorable reputation benefits a company in a number of ways. It:

- influences how financial markets evaluate a publicly held company[44]
- enables a firm to charge premium prices[45]
- influences buying intentions and decisions[46]
- achieves sustainable competitive advantage[47]
- enhances financial performance[48]
- signals quality of products and strategies compared to rivals[49]
- provides clues about future and new product performance[50]
- increases customer loyalty[51]
- improves beliefs in advertising[52]
- attracts and retains employees[53] and investors
- indicates resolve in situations of distress

Not recognizing the importance of reputation can be costly. Recent surveys show that reputation loss poses the greatest overall threat to an organization[54] and its market value[55] and is the sixth most significant threat to a company's earnings.[56] Moreover, events that damage a firm's reputation have been known to result in a 25 percent loss of share value following the disclosure of the event.[57] The following graphs stress the casualties of reputation risk events.

Morgan Stanley *(market value loss of $11 billion)*

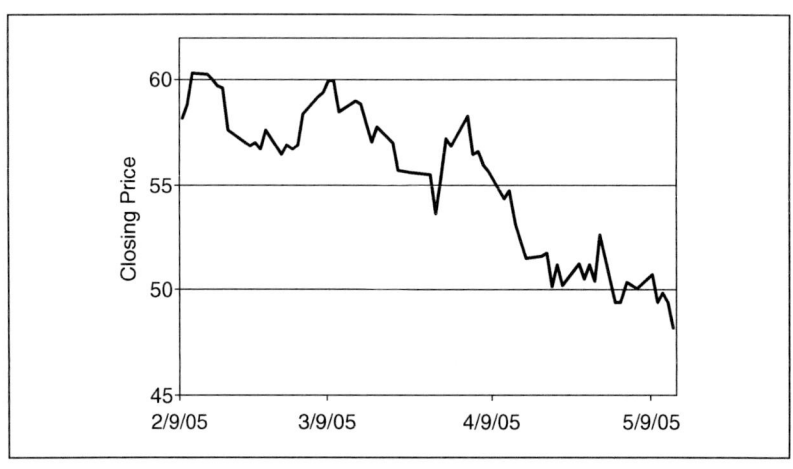

In July 2004, Morgan Stanley agreed to pay $54 million to settle a sex discrimination lawsuit accusing the firm of denying equal pay and promotions to women. Alumni publicly berated the company for change after additional internal issues were identified. The challenges at Morgan Stanley caused the NYSE to impose a $19 million dollar fine for regulatory and supervisory lapses. The subsequent stock drop of 17 percent created unrest inside and outside the company that caused many executives to leave.

Complaints filed against ChoicePoint, a provider of fraud prevention information and technology solutions, allege executives misrepresented the company's financial condition and knew the security measures designed to protect consumers from security breaches were inadequate and ineffective. The security breaches resulted in the loss of hundreds of thousands of consumers' data records. These events resulted in: the discontinuance of some product sales, reducing company rev-

ChoicePoint *(market value loss of $1 billion)*

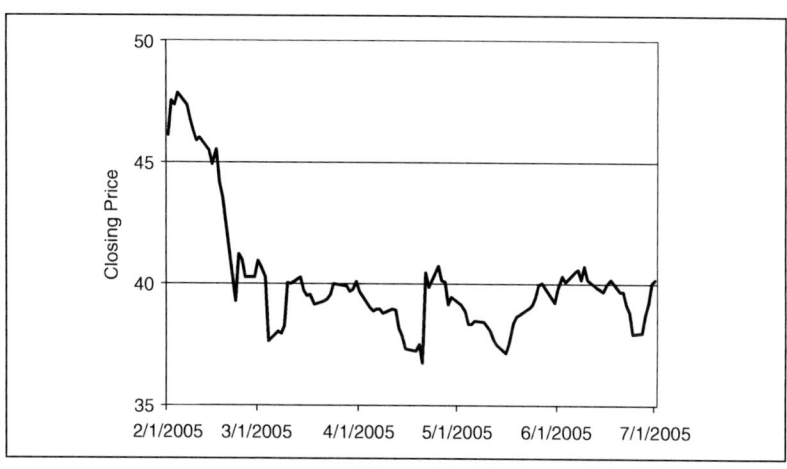

enues by $15 to $20 million, SEC inquiries of executive stock sales made before the 2004–2005 breach was made public, and increased legislator and regulatory interest to pass customer notification laws when a data security breach occurs.

Managing Reputation Risk. The media is littered with information that shapes our impressions and opinions of an organization and its practices (including products and services). Reputation is not always formed based on direct or indirect experiences. In many cases, perception is reality.

Although there has been extensive research about reputation, the formal topic of reputation risk management has similar recognition as other risk management disciplines. In fact, the few reputation risk management techniques that have been explored[58] mirror generic underlying risk management principles. Moreover, there is not a universally agreed on definition of or approach to managing reputation risk. Nevertheless, one theme does permeate the literature: managing reputation risk requires some degree of subjectivity and professional judgment.

For our purposes, *reputation risk is the reduced market value or constituent perception as a result of an organization's or its competitors' past, current, or future business practices.*

Crisis Management. The topic of reputation risk management would be incomplete without a brief synopsis of managing crises. Ideally, effective reputation risk management should focus on the proactive—assessing what could happen and what the outcomes might be. Having made such assessments improves a bank's ability to react during a crisis—and the ability to react well in times of crisis can influence an organization's reputation.

For example, when containers of Johnson & Johnson's Tylenol were found to contain cyanide and caused several deaths, the company recognized the value of protecting consumers' safety. It immediately pulled the product off the shelves and stopped production. Afterwards, Johnson & Johnson ran ad campaigns announcing its intentions and redesigned the product's seal. Within three months, it had regained 95 percent of its precrisis market share and arguably strengthened its reputation.

Crisis management can be broadly structured as follows:

Anticipate: What possible surprises can happen to the organization? Using risk assessment framework, scenario planning, and encouraging employee perspectives are all useful ways to ferret out threats.

Prepare: Detail how to respond to a crisis. Typically, this involves creating a crisis-management plan, which is broader than the typical business continuity plan. The plan defines roles and responsibilities of who does what and when.

Identify: Know when the organization is in a crisis. This requires a pulse on others' comments and perceptions.

Respond: Once a crisis has occurred, respond quickly and honestly. For example:

- State the facts of the situation, keep them relevant, and tailor them to each stakeholder. Convey all bad news as soon as possible in jargon-free communication.
- Ensure the most senior executive responds, preferably at the scene. This shows credibility and caring.
- Monitor and manage media activity and address significant and relevant inaccuracies.
- Have a single spokesperson for the organization.

Update the crisis management plan periodically and ensure that employees are aware of their responsibilities.

Summary of Reputation Risk. Banks create enormous benefits and value through their reputations. In essence, banks must protect their reputations. The ability for the organization to formalize a structured approach to manage reputation risk enables it to proactively identify and address issues that can deteriorate confidence, financial performance, and, in the worst cases, its solvency.

A bank may not have to change its management approach if the infrastructure exists. It may be as simple as integrating subject matter expertise, aggregating information from internal functions, and leveraging existing processes and tools. As banks grow and become more diversified, a central reputation risk management function can act as a vital intermediary. Reputation is tied to the entire company, not its parts.

Regulatory Risk

According to the Basel Committee on Banking Supervision, regulatory risk (compliance risk) is defined as the *risk of legal or regulatory sanctions, financial loss or the loss to reputation a bank may suffer as a result of its failure to comply with applicable laws, regulations, codes of conduct and standards of good practice.*[59] Simply put, it is the risk associated with the failure to comply with laws related to banking and related practices.

Consumer compliance regulations, the Bank Secrecy Act, and the Community Reinvestment Act constitute some of the more fundamental, significant, genres of regulations for any bank.

Because the banking industry is one of the most heavily regulated, regulatory risks are one of the most significant risks to any bank. Ever changing banking laws result in additional regulatory risks, which considerably influence the bank's operations. Failure to comply with regulatory changes may result in censure and significant fines and penalties.

Therefore, the principal goal of a bank's regulatory-risk program is to provide proactive and ongoing monitoring and assurance regarding compliance with all internal policies and procedures as well as with applicable laws and regulations. The key words are "proactive" and "on-going." It is important that the process be both proactive and ongoing because it is a risk management function, not an internal-audit function that is both periodic and reactive (see chapter 4).

The lack of an effective regulatory-risk program exposes the bank to the possibility that a banking regulator may disapprove merger or other expansion plans. In evaluating merger or expansion applications, banking regulators also assess the effectiveness of the board and management to identify, assess, manage, and monitor risk. Weak risk management (or regulatory risk management) programs ultimately reflect poorly on the board and management.

Defining the Job. Senior management has established most traditional compliance functions as an oversight task ensuring compliance with laws and regulations as well as internal policies. This traditional role is, however, changing. Recent high-profile governance failures and the increasing complexities of emerging regulations demand a more robust compliance function and greater collaboration between the bank's top compliance officer and managers at all levels of the institution.

In order to accommodate the increasing importance of the compliance function, banks have begun to question themselves: Is management spending enough or too much to manage our regulatory risk? What qualitative assessment tools are currently in place and are they effective? What quantitative assessment tools can be employed to assess the likelihood and severity of compliance failures?

Though there are no clear answers to these questions, banks have nevertheless defined the bank's compliance risks, significantly increased their compliance staff, applied a risk-based approach (and additional funds) for training, controls, and independent testing, and consolidated the compliance function under risk management.[60]

In anticipation of regulatory compliance reviews, the most astute compliance officers incorporate the regulatory examination procedures into their ongoing monitoring and assessment function. The scope of a review is a function of the breadth and complexity of the institution's products, the inherent risk in those products, and the bank's history of compliance and effectively implementing previously mandated corrective actions.

And while all regulations are created equal under the law, the fact is that certain regulations possess a higher degree of risk due to the significant penalties of noncompliance. In this regard, the following chart (exhibit 6.3, from the 2002 Federal Reserve Bank of Kansas City's white paper "A Banker's Guide to Establishing Compliance Management Program"[61]) is used by the Fed's compliance examiners to help scope their reviews.

Other, more recent high-risk regulations should include the:

- Bank Secrecy Act
- Patriot Act
- Anti-Money Laundering Regulations
- Fair and Accurate Credit Transactions (FACT) Act
- Home Mortgage Disclosure Act (HMDA)

One simple practice that is easily implemented and will certainly help mitigate regulatory risks is to include the bank's

EXHIBIT 6.3 Regulatory Risk Table

Risk	Statute/Regulation	Section(s) of Statute/Regulation
(Low) 1	Real Estate Settlement Procedures Act (Reg X)	Mortgage Servicing Transfer Disclosure
	Right To Financial Privacy Act	All
	Fair Debt Collections Practices Act	All
	Unfair or Deceptive Acts or Practices (Reg AA)	All
	Rule of 78s	All
	Fair Credit Reporting Act	All
2	Expedited Funds Availability Act (Reg CC)	All
	Truth in Savings Act (Reg DD)	All
	Reserve Requirements (Reg D)	All
	Consumer Leasing (Reg M)	All
	Interest on Deposits (Reg Q)	All
3	Real Estate Settlement Procedures Act (Reg X)	All provisions except those rated "1"
	National Flood Insurance Act (Reg H)	All
	Truth in Lending Act (Reg Z)	All provisions except those rated "4"
	Electronic Funds Transfer Act (Reg E)	All
	Fair Lending (Other Reg B and FHA Provisions)	Technical provisions
(High) 4	Truth in Lending Act (Reg Z)	APR/Finance Charge and Rescission

compliance officers in developing and introducing new products. In doing so, potential violations may be mitigated before they occur, and precious time and money may be saved by not having to retune or redesign the product or campaign.

Culture and Structure. The overall structure of regulatory risk departments does not vary significantly from bank to bank. Most departments include a staff of compliance officers and a small staff of other risk managers to conduct independent reviews of BSA and data integrity tests of CRA and HMDA data. Nevertheless, the structure of the regulatory risk department will vary depending on the size and complexity of the bank's products, services, and operations.[62]

Regardless of the structure, regulatory risk management must be integrated fully into the bank's ERM program. Like other risks, regulatory risk is not unique unto itself. Regulatory risks are found throughout the organization and very often influence other types and sources of risk, particularly credit and operational risks. Although credit, market, and operational risks may expose the bank to explicit losses, the failure to manage regulatory risk can result in severe fines and can derail business strategies, resulting in very significant loss in terms of management time and effort.

Governance. Many banks also have established compliance committees as a way to integrate the regulatory-risk function into the day-to-day management of the bank. These committees review risk management reports, provide a forum for discussing existing and emerging regulatory risks, ensure that adverse findings are promptly and effectively corrected, and review policies and procedures that give rise to regulatory risks. This committee should have the full support of senior management, and periodic reports of the committee's activities should be made to the board audit- or risk-management committee.

Federal banking regulators are adopting a "top down" approach to supervision. In short, the regulators want to see clear and compelling evidence that a bank has a strong compliance culture supported by the appropriate "tone at the top." Recently, the Federal Reserve opined on the importance of a strong compliance culture, backed by senior management and the board, and the need to avoid thinking of regulatory risk assessment as a cost center.[63]

As federal banking regulators continue to shift toward a risk-based, top-down, supervisory approach, their focus will predictably shift to the bank's systems, processes, controls, and management's reports. This shift will further highlight the importance of internal regulatory risk assessments, monitoring, and reporting.

Ultimately, compliance with law, regulations, policies, and procedure is the responsibility of every employee. As such, compliance responsibility should be integrated openly into the bank's corporate culture, and employees whose jobs affect compliance performance should be held accountable.

Role of the Compliance Officer. The role and importance of the corporate compliance function continues to expand and, as a result, executive peers and other managers may not fully understand the role of a compliance officer or the role of the compliance function. Should the compliance officer be a neutral arbitrator and adjudicator, or should he or she be more of an administrator, supervisor, and emissary of management and the board? The answer is all of the above.

Usually a bank's compliance officer is the regulatory risk liaison between management and federal banking regulators. For this reason, the compliance officer is typically a senior officer of the bank. As such, a compliance officer must build relationships throughout the company and with the board and regulators as well. He or she must assess and manage the risks and costs of the company's compliance efforts. As such, it is critical to empower a compliance officer with the authority to require and enforce compliance with policies, procedures, and regulations.

A bank's compliance officer also must develop a long-term, strategic-level view of a bank's compliance program. This "compliance plan" must be well defined and holistic; it must consider the impact on other types of risk; it must be risk-based and consider and anticipate the sources of compliance failures; and it must be built around a value-building strategy.

Compliance programs that are flexible and supported by a strong organizational culture will more easily accommodate and support organizational change.

Depending on the size, complexity, and nature of unresolved regulatory issues, a compliance officer's day-to-day activities and priorities may vary significantly. In order for a compliance program to succeed, a compliance officer must be kept abreast of high-priority issues and must be flexible enough to change gears in response to ever-changing priorities.

Managing the regulatory risk function is similar to managing many other functions of the bank. Compliance officers often must make the most effective use of limited resources and must direct attention to the most critical (highest risk) areas first. In doing so, the compliance officer must bring to senior management's and the board's attention those situations that present the bank with a higher degree of risk. Particularly, when ongoing assessments conclude that past weaknesses and repeat violations persist, the compliance officer must report the situation to the highest levels of management and to the board's audit or risk committee.

Because the compliance function is not entirely a police function, the compliance officer also must develop and implement a program that devotes significant attention to ongoing training and research and promotes participation in various committees and planning sessions, particularly where new products or changes to related operating procedures are involved.

One of the most important roles of the compliance officer is to promote and ensure a good working relationship with federal banking regulators. Unfortunately, when compliance failures are abundant and a bank's compliance program is week, the traditional regulatory relationship may become adversarial.

Furthermore, the combination of continually changing regulations and increased regulatory focus on systems and controls has led to changing benchmarks of expectations and accepted best practices from the banking regulators. Compliance officers therefore should be experts in consumer regulations and should keep management and the board up-to-date on changes in regulations and emerging issues.

For this reason, if for no other, it is essential to engage banking regulators in frequent and open dialogue on both ongoing and emerging issues. Likewise, regulators expect to be informed of significant developments at the institution before learning about it from the press. Simply put, both the bank and its regulators do not want to be surprised. If banks and their regulators want to establish a collaborative working relationship with each other, then both must make every effort to communicate openly and constructively with each another.

A first step to ensure a cordial working relationship with bank regulators is to take examination findings seriously but not personally. The compliance officer must ensure that all examination findings are communicated and adequately, and promptly, addressed. Senior management and the board also must remember that virtually all examinations result in a list of items warranting management's attention. It is a serious mistake to dismiss these issues as merely technical issues of the day and relegate responsibility for addressing them to either the compliance or internal audit functions. Few things upset banking regulators more than to find that issues identified during their most recent review were hardly addressed or, worse yet, summarily dismissed.

Independence. With respect to independence, the FDIC Compliance Handbook states: "It is important that the duties and responsibilities are clearly defined and include accessibility to both the board and senior management. The compliance officer or committee should report directly to the board or chief executive officer. It is important that the designated individual(s) be provided sufficient authority and independence to implement policies and institute corrective action."[64]

Investment companies and investment advisers are now required by recent SEC regulation to have a compliance officer with significant independence from the company's executive leadership. The recently enacted regulations state that the "compliance officer will report directly to the [fund's] board of directors." The regulation goes on to state that the board of directors must review and approve the fund's compliance officer, including compensation.[65]

The appropriate reporting lines therefore serve to prevent conflicts of interest. Whether or not it is articulated in a regulatory handbook or other publication, preventing conflicts of interest is a matter of common sense. Furthermore, budget constraints by management also will compromise both the independence and effectiveness of the compliance function.

However, where the bank's compliance officer wears more than one hat, great care should be taken to ensure that the compliance officer is not also conducting reviews of his or her own work. For example, if the compliance officer is also the bank's BSA officer, then he or she cannot conduct the independent testing of this function.

It is important at this point to note that independence has a dual meaning for the compliance function. First, the function must be sufficiently independent to have a reporting relationship to the board of directors. Second, and more importantly, the function must be independent of the process being reviewed.

Nevertheless, senior managers and the board should bear in mind that whereas independent testing is fundamental to the function, making sure that all unresolved issues are promptly and effectively corrected is critical.

Summary of Regulatory Risk. Constantly changing banking laws pose an ever-increasing regulatory risk to a bank. Failure to comply with regulatory changes may result in censure and significant fines and penalties.

The frequency and scope of independent testing should be predicated on the degree of risk to the bank; that is, the greater the risk, the more frequent and thorough the testing, and the greater the internal controls required.

Regulatory risk management must be supported from the top and fully integrated into the bank's overall compliance culture and risk management program.

The compliance officer must develop a clear and holistic compliance plan that not only address current and emerging compliance issues but also is built around a value-building strategy. Furthermore, to be successful, the compliance officer must develop and nurture a close working relationship with the bank's regulators. One of the most important aspects of an effective compliance program is to make all employees, in a sense, compliance officers and therefore accountable for compliance. The belief that ensuring regulatory compliance is the compliance officer's job is an absolute guarantee of violations.

The necessary independence of the compliance function is not only intuitive but mandated by regulators. Nevertheless, compliance also is a management function. As such, the duties and responsibilities of the compliance officer must be well-defined and include accessibility to both the board and senior management. Independence aside, it is more important to ensure that all unresolved regulatory compliance issues are promptly and effectively remedied.

Strategic Risk

One thing a person cannot do, no matter how rigorous his analysis or heroic his imagination, is to draw up a list of things that would never occur to him.
Thomas Schelling, professor emeritus, Harvard University

Traditional strategic planning develops missions, vision, goals, strategies, tactics, timeframes, and so forth for the bank. Sometimes strategic planning can produce ideas for new products. However, traditional strategic planning is typically not "strategic" at all; it is a manager's written and graphical expression of how he or she runs the business and therefore reflects the status quo.

Federal Reserve Governor Susan Schmidt Bies suggests that banks move away from building the strategic plan with a most-likely future and stretch it to consider alternative outcomes.[66] In so doing, the bank's management incorporates the risk decision making into the planning process.

Various tools have arisen in the past few decades from many consulting firms to make traditional strategic planning more "strategic." These tools carry a variety of names and most, if not all, have the two purposes of ERM built within: seeking a positive outcome while mitigating the negative possibilities. This affirms the notion that ERM is a strategic business decision, and strategic risk may therefore be defined as: *the risks associated with business decisions—such as acquisitions, new product launches, new technologies, and market shifts—that impact the brand.*[67]

OPERATIONAL RISK EVALUATION TOOLS

As previously discussed, VAR provides the bank executive with a metric for unexpected loss. Problematic in that approach is actually having the historical data with which to calculate that metric. Since VAR calculations are based on that data, management must find other ways in which to assess and control operational risks. Routine assessments of operational risk sub-components, such as legal risk, reputation risk, regulatory risk, and strategic risk, may provide a more undemanding, albeit a less fully integrated, method of quantifiably managing operational risk.

Operational Risk Management's Iterative Process

Three key risk management principles establish the foundation for evaluating operational risks:

1. identify
2. assess
3. evaluate

These principles form an iterative process, as exhibit 6.4 illustrates.

Since organizations live in a dynamic business and operating environment, in order to remain competitive, an organization is forced to perform different activities from rivals or to perform similar activities in different ways. These changing conditions create new risks that require stakeholders to be diligent in their management techniques.

Identify. Identifying operational risk requires defining and understanding the interests of the bank's constituent population:

- ➤ *Customers and Consumers:* What discourages repeat purchases or reduces market share?
- ➤ *Employees:* What makes jobs less attractive or de-motivates employees?

EXHIBIT 6.4 Operational Risk Management's Iterative Process

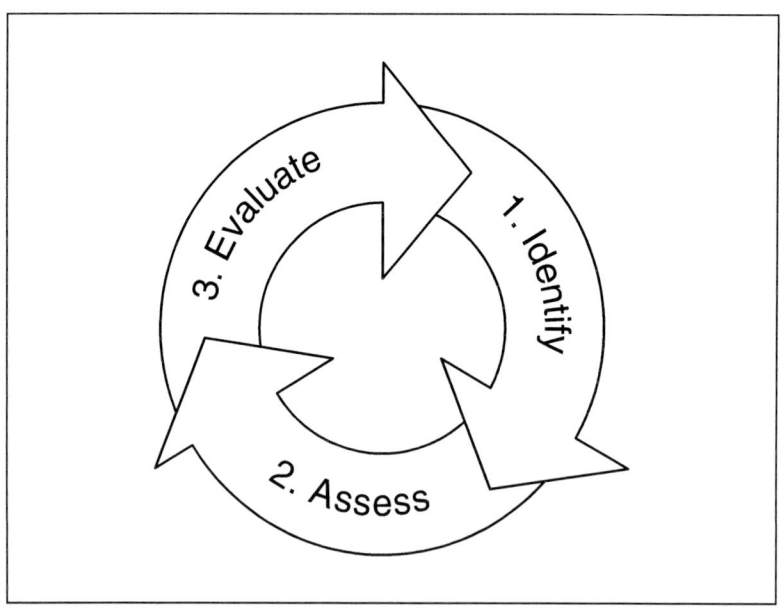

- *Stakeholder advocacy groups:* What encourages engagement or interest?
- *Regulatory and legislative bodies:* What heightens awareness or action?
- *Investors/analysts:* What increases capital costs, negatively affects analyst coverage and content, or detracts from new investment?
- *Media:* What provokes negative television, press, or Web content?
- *Suppliers/third parties:* What external relationship activities create organizational distress?

A rather low-tech method for identifying the risk in this manner is to do something very simple with the constituent population: ask them.

A proven and effective method for achieving operational risk identification (and sometimes credit and market risks as well) is to ask the constituent population what negative consequences exist. In other words, what are the negative things that could, might, will, or already have happened—either to the bank, the competition, or the industry?

Set no limits. Allow the group—a group will give much more objective answers than an individual—to list as many negative aspects of the operation as they can. After the list is complete, depending on time constraints, the group should pick its top issues from the list. By examining each issue, management can get a fairly complete picture of the operational risks of most concern within the organization.

Assess. Once the prioritized list exists, the next step is to ask the group how negative is negative? Is it a minor inconvenience or a bank killer or somewhere in between? Once there is consensus on the magnitude or impact of that item, the group should assess what it views as the likelihood of that risk occurring.

In order to truly quantify the risk, the bank executive should quantify the impact and the likelihood. Rather than state that the magnitude of a risk, if it were to happen, is "minor," state a dollar loss or a market capitalization reduction. Rather than state that the probability of a risk occurring is remote, state that it has a 5 percent or less chance of happening. Exhibit 6.5 shows an example of the quantification.

It is not important that management copy the ranges as they appear in exhibit 6.5, just that they define the ranges before the assessment. Once the exercise is completed, they will find the operational risks quantified in the "matrix"[68] illustrated in exhibit 6.6.

Evaluate. Risk identification and assessment provide the basis for evaluating whether and how to develop management strategies. In their simplest form, the options are straightforward:

- Retain or accept the risk.
- Mitigate the risk (controls and/or insurance).
- Refrain from the practice.

Determining which management strategy to choose requires an analysis of whether the costs of risk outweigh the benefits. What happens if the risk were to occur? Did the risk assessment yield the appropriate concerns to enable the organization to make the correct decision?

EXHIBIT 6.5 Quantification of Operational Risks

Risk Level	Impact	Likelihood
High	Corporate "Death Penalty" (loss or fine equal to the bank's net worth)	Imminent (75% to 100% probability of occurrence)
Medium	Loss/fine equal to 30% to 60% of the bank's net worth	50/50 chance of occurrence
Low	Loss/fine less than 10% of the bank's net worth	Remote (very little chance of happening)

EXHIBIT 6.6 The Risk Manager's Impact-Likelihood Matrix

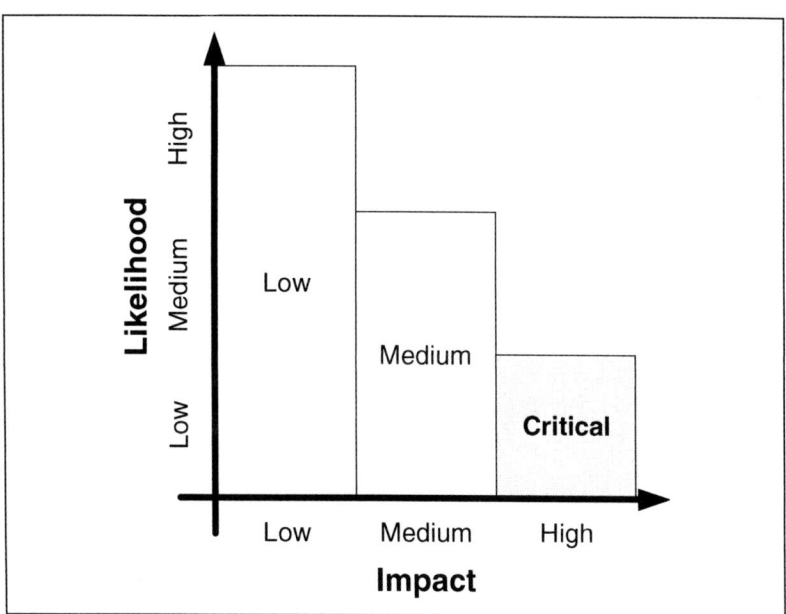

Putting the Tools to Work

In reviewing some of the major operational risk categories covered in this chapter, a bank executive can use the impact-likelihood matrix as detailed in the following paragraphs.

Legal Risk Evaluation. Financial institutions have a disproportionably high level of inherent legal risk. At both the state and federal level, banking is a highly regulated industry. As an unintended consequence or lack of internal and external oversight, banks may violate regulatory laws and regulations, state consumer protection statutes, competitive practices (antitrust), state licensing rules, privacy rules, money laundering reporting and enforcement, and many more. Identifying and measuring these risks likely will be more subjective than the other risk categories discussed earlier. The complexity of the business and the jurisdictions in which a bank operates may influence a banker's awareness of these risks. Nevertheless, the bank's counsel should develop and maintain a report identifying outstanding legal issues and note his or her best estimate of the possible outcome and impact of each issue to the bank (exhibit 6.7).

Reputation Risk Evaluation. This definition of reputation risk—*the reduced market value or constituent perception as a result of an organization's or its competitors' past, current, or future business practices*—establishes the foundation for the key operational risk management principles mentioned earlier in this chapter:

1. identify
2. assess
3. evaluate

Identify. Identifying reputation risk is not simple. As in any other operational risk, it requires defining and understanding the interests of the organization's constituent population. Management must be able to understand the cues that the organization's constituents consider in forming a corporate reputation in order to effectively assess risk. Many of these constituent groups align to existing organizational functions (for example,

EXHIBIT 6.7 Legal Risks Impact-Likelihood Matrix

First National Bank vs. XYZ Creditor		
Risk Level	Impact	Likelihood
High	$0 to $500K	Imminent (75% to 100% probability of occurrence)
Medium	$501K to $1MM	50/50 chance of occurrence
Low	$1MM+	Remote (very little chance of happening)

employee interests may be understood by Human Resources). As a result, the reputation risk management group should interact with each function to leverage employee subject-matter expertise and/or other existing tools in these functions to form a more complete picture of the risk.

Accompanying the risks identified by constituent functions are those identified by the business itself. Reputation risks, like other risks, can be identified through risk self-assessments. This occurs when management assesses its operations, products, practices, environment, and so forth to determine how reputation risk affects its business model and objectives. Each line of business may have a different viewpoint than the risk management function. Therefore, it is crucial that management have the tools and resources necessary to identify reputation risk proactively and efficiently. It is the responsibility of every employee to protect and enhance the reputation of the organization.

Depending on the risk management infrastructure of the organization, the business may require education on what reputation risk is, what the desired reputation of the company is, and constituent concerns. Typically, this requires some initial training, and it requires sustained processes/tools so the business is able to identify the reputation risks dynamically as the environment or marketplace changes. This may be as simple as requiring dynamic self-assessments for significant changes in the business, such as new/changed products, processes, and so forth, or maintaining an "issue list" of each constituent's concerns on the organization's intranet.

Other sources of risk identification include information from audit reports, scenario analysis/planning, benchmarks, competitive information, observations from legislative and regulatory activity, analyst reports, legal and court proceedings, and media sources. Additionally, other risk management functions may garner information about future reputation risk events (for example, compliance violations may spur regulatory interest, and operational breakdowns could agitate customers).

Management may identify risks in such a way that they fall into independent categories (or silos). For example, a risk may be classified as either a legal risk or a reputation risk, but not both. This monotonic classification of risk may cause significant reputation risks to go unnoticed. Therefore, the risk management functions must work collaboratively. This has two benefits: identified risks are shared to ensure significant risks are analyzed from all perspectives, and senior managers are better able to view the risk holistically and do not receive information through disparate channels.

For reputation risk management to be successful, risk management, constituent, and business process functions should be supported by effective information and communication. However, this network will be fundamentally incomplete if the organization does not have grounding in a sound corporate culture and value system that is understood by all its employees.[69]

Assess. Once a reputation risk is identified, it should be assessed to determine its repercussion. Assessing reputation risk is similar to other accepted risk management methodologies (i.e., both likelihood and severity, as mentioned above).

The variables that go into determining the exposure of a particular reputation risk are frequently subjective, may vary with organizational imperatives, and do not easily lend themselves to quantification. However, encouraging the organization to assess risk in tangible terms will enhance analysis, benchmarking, and reporting.

Likelihood is assessed on how probable the risk is to occur. Estimating the likelihood of reputation risk may be challenging. However, it may be possible to codify some estimates. For example, tracking negative mentions of the organization or competitors in the press (newspapers, legislative meetings, analyst comments, and so forth) can be modeled for trends about industry scrutiny or particular business practices. Similarly, monitoring call centers for adverse customer experiences may signal decreases in satisfaction.

Impact is the exposure to the company (either in quantitative or qualitative terms) should the risk occur. The impact to the organization could be tied to different variables for each constituent group. These could include varying levels of media exposure (local, national, international), the attention and action of advocacy groups, regulators, and investors, the impact on employee morale, lost customers, and customer complaints.

As part of the assessment step, the reputation risk management function should act as a conduit between the business and the constituent subject matter experts, to facilitate a more robust and thorough discussion about the risk. Understanding, for example, that a product's features (1) are a common platform for vocal advocacy groups, (2) are a hot topic for attorneys general, (3) have attracted significant negative press about a similar, competitive product, and (4) have resulted in a recent increase in customer complaints, may result in a more accurate assessment of the risk.

Plotting this into a risk matrix, as depicted in exhibit 6.8, sets a forum for discussion. If a particular risk is determined to have a low likelihood of occurrence and a medium impact, the assessment should not be taken verbatim. It is important to understand the underlying criteria and logic for the assessment.

For example, it may be imperative for an organization to increase customer satisfaction. Let's say the business identifies a reputation risk to this imperative and assesses it as having low exposure. Subject matter experts representing the constituent groups also assess this risk. On average, all constituent groups (except the consumer constituent group) assess the risk as low-to-moderate exposure. The consumer constituent group rates the risk as critical. For this particular risk, the consumer constituent group may have a greater weight placed on its assessment. Hence, once these distinct assessments are discussed, this risk may be deemed to have an overall higher exposure. Although ownership of risk management usually lies within the business, a dichotomy may exist between how

Exhibit 6.8 Preliminary and Aggregated Reputation Risk Matrices

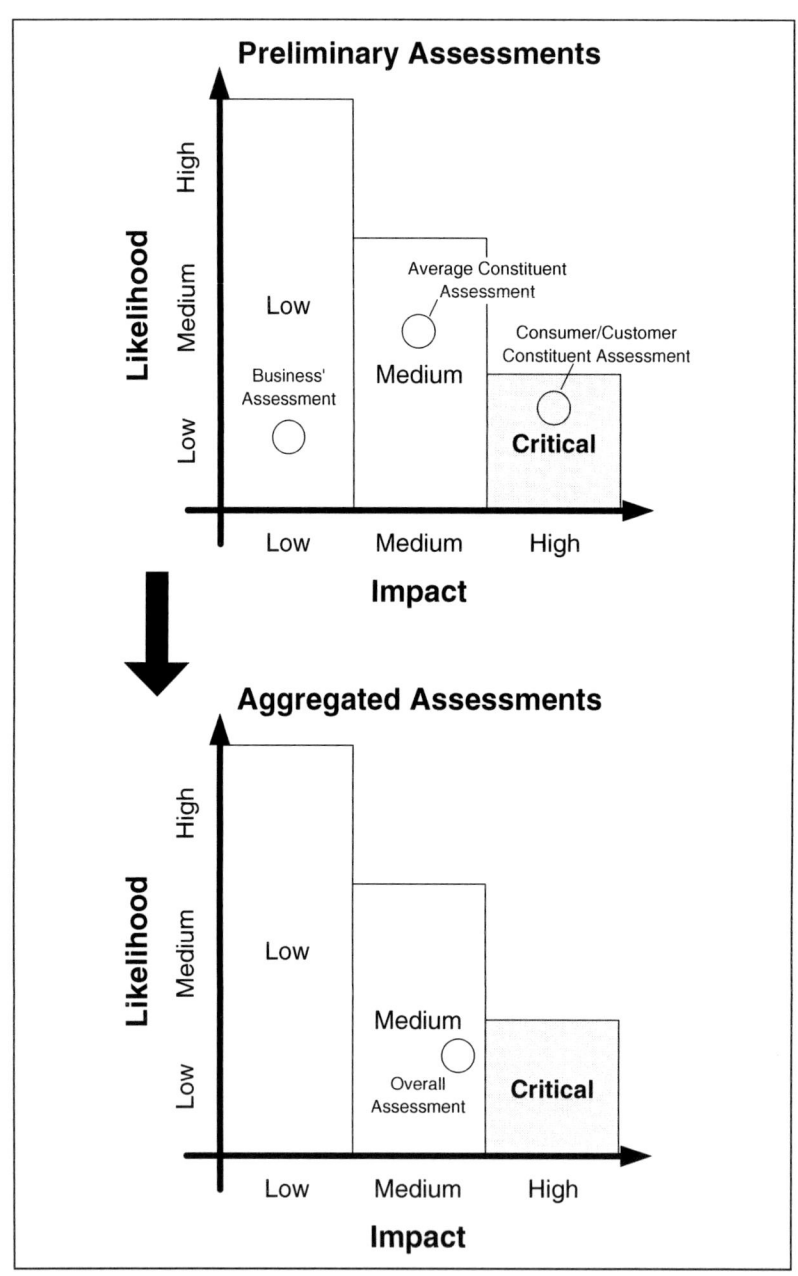

much risk the business is willing to take and how much the organization is willing to accept.

Evaluate. In its simplest form, the options are to retain, mitigate, or avoid the risk/practice. Management also can continually reassess a particular risk to see whether more information about the risk leads to a more educated assessment of the risk.

Determining which management strategy to choose requires an analysis of whether the costs of a risk outweigh its benefits. What happens if the risk were to occur? Did the assessment of the risk yield the appropriate concerns to enable the organization to make the correct decision?

A recent study[70] looked at the impact of risk events on the market value of banks and insurance companies. The study found the response of stock values to risk losses to be substantially greater than one-for-one, implying such events convey adverse information about future cash flows and extend beyond the amount of the losses themselves. Moreover, the study suggests loss events may serve as signals of poor management quality and operational controls. This can be further illustrated by New York Attorney General Eliot Spitzer's actions against Marsh & McLennan, where he accused the firm of bid rigging and cheating clients. After the probe was announced, Marsh & McLennan's market value dropped roughly 50 percent or close to $12 billion. A few months later, Marsh & McLennan agreed to pay $850 million in restitution.

Granted, our looking at examples like the above (Enron, Arthur Andersen, AIG, and so forth) may be using aberrations to stress testing assessments, but nevertheless such risks do occur. Regardless, the experience of other organizations (both in industry and out) should act as possible signals for determining the proper course of action.

Reputation risk is unique from other risk management disciplines because of the subjectivity involved in making an evaluative decision. Organizations frequently only see the upside of taking risk and typically dismiss the nominal financial effect that controls have on determining net present values of projects. This back-of-the-envelope approach to managing risk may result in dire consequences.

Ultimately, the goal of the entire framework should be to initiate the process early. This will enable an organization to alleviate wasting resources and capital for those initiatives it wants to avoid because of the high reputation exposure.

Scenario Analysis

Scenario analysis introduces the risk management element into corporate America's strategic planning process. Ben Carson, the gifted pediatric neurosurgeon at Johns Hopkins hospital, sits on a number of corporate boards of directors. When asked how he can contribute to the seemingly unrelated disciplines of both medicine and business, Dr. Carson replied that, in the operating room as well as in the board room, he asks four questions before making a big decision: "What is the best thing that happens if I do something? What is the worst thing that happens if I do something? What is the best thing that happens when I do nothing? What is the worst thing that happens when I do nothing?"[71]

Those four simple—and sometimes life and death—questions illustrate another way by which management may analyze and measure risk: scenario analysis. This approach, illustrated in exhibit 6.9, is a lot less mathematically intensive than those described earlier.

Those four questions assist management and the board in determining not only the risk appetite of a bank for a new venture or product, but also a risk versus reward trade-off. If a bank is contemplating a choice between acquiring an existing bank charter or starting a *de novo* bank in that same market, for example, the Outcomes Matrix may look like exhibit 6.10 below.

Management would ask the same four questions about starting a *de novo* bank.

EXHIBIT 6.9 Outcomes Matrix

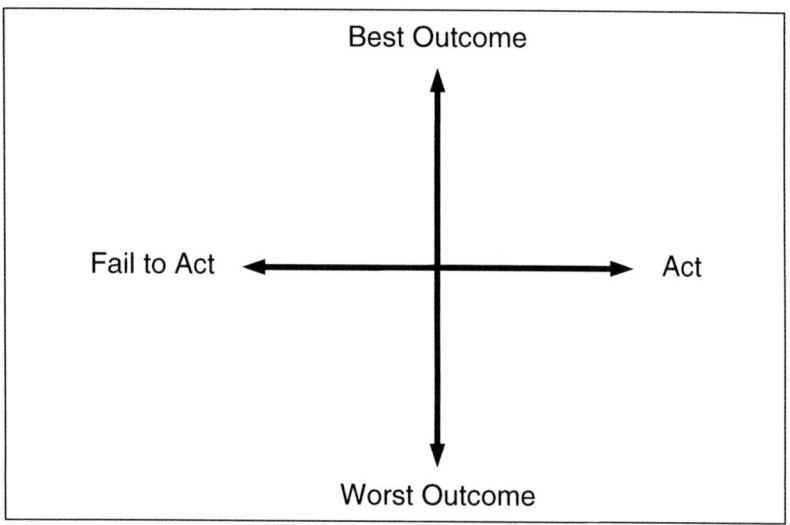

EXHIBIT 6.10 Outcomes Matrix—Potential Acquisition

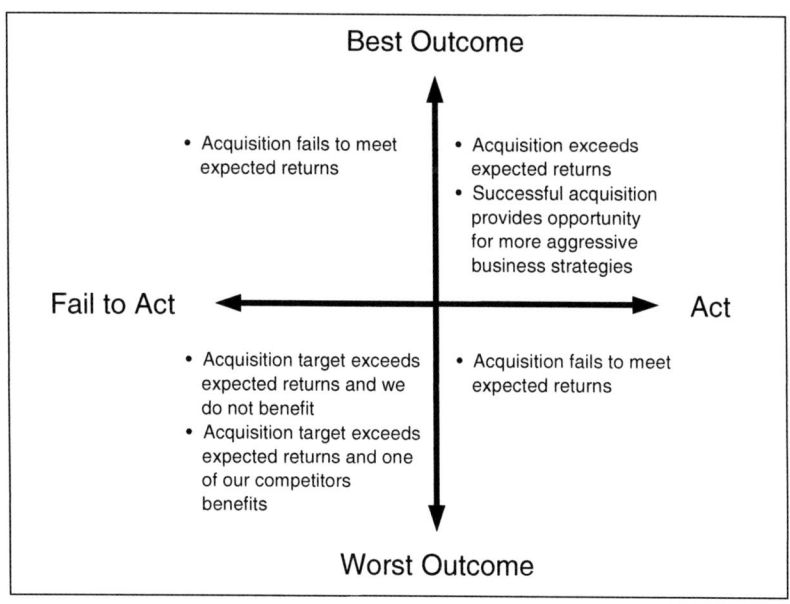

CONCLUSION

Banks are discovering that operational risk management goes well beyond simply emphasizing attentiveness and rehearsing control procedures in the hope that an effective operational risk management program will inevitably develop. Management, and indeed all employees, must first understand that everyone in the bank serves as an operational risk manager.

To build an effective operational-risk function, management must:

- clearly identify and assess the bank's operational risks
- involve all stakeholders
- extensively and continuously test the bank's system of internal controls
- adopt processes designed to measure and monitor changes in expected and unexpected losses in correlation to their controls
- constantly evaluate the risk versus reward trade-off

VAR provides management with a single number that can be used to summarize information about the operational risk of the bank or across various operational lines of business. The lack of robust loss data may inhibit management by VAR; however, dividing operational risk into its various subcomponents and assessing each individually can still be an effective means of managing operational risk.

Regardless of the methodology employed, implementing an efficient operational risk management program will produce many tangible benefits, including a reduction in losses, increases in profitability, and ultimately enhanced shareholder value.

Key Points
Operational Risk

- Effective operational risk management requires a significant effort.
- An organization must identify and assess its risks, assign them to owners, objectively measure the quality of internal controls, and monitor changes in risk levels and controls.
- Expected loss is the amount of money a business loses on average in one year. Unexpected loss is the amount a business could lose in a bad year in excess of the budget for expected loss.
- The calculation of the unexpected loss is the amount a bank should reserve as capital.
- When assessing operational risk, management should quantify the impact of the adverse consequences of the risk.

PART 3

INTEGRATING ERM INTO THE ORGANIZATION

Typically, economic capital is allocated to the risk trinity: credit risk, market risk, and operational risk. The key approach to managing these risks has been discussed in Parts 1 and 2. This final section focuses on some simple quantitative measurements of risk and on allocating economic capital.

Measuring risk using quantitative processes such as calculating VAR and RAROC informs management of the *level* of credit, market, or operational risks. Economic capital calculations allow management to compare relatively disparate risks to each other, across the risk trinity.

Ultimately the fundamental goal of risk management is to employ both qualitative and quantitative processes, in an efficient and effective manner, in order to identify, assess, and manage risk by managing economic capital. Terms such as "high," "moderate," or "low" risk can be too subjective. In response, VAR, Risk-Adjusted Return on Capital (RAROC) (explained in chapter 8) and economic capital have become part of the common language for risk practitioners around the world. As such, measuring and managing risk in these terms is paramount.

Chapter 7 highlights different quantitative methodologies used in measuring risk.

Chapter 8 discusses economic capital and ways in which it may be applied across products or lines of business in order to measure risk-adjusted performance and returns. Armed with this knowledge, management can then maximize shareholder value by reallocating capital to those products or lines-of-business with greater and more sustainable economic returns.

Chapter 7

INTEGRATING BANK RISKS THROUGH MEASUREMENT

Truth is truth to the end of reckoning.
William Shakespeare (1564–1616),
Measure for Measure, Act V. Sc. 1.

During World War II, shortages abounded, particularly with the U.S. Armed Forces' airplane mechanics. Consequently, they did not have enough armor to cover the entire undercarriages of all aircraft to protect them from anti-aircraft fire. Instead, the repair mechanics had to determine exactly where to place scarce armor to protect as much of the vulnerable areas of the fuselage as possible.

They had no way to tell where the vulnerabilities were from downed aircraft. But rather than pour over the schematics of each aircraft, trying to determine the vulnerabilities in the design and calculating probabilities of mortal hits, they simply studied the damage on returning aircraft. If it was hit in a certain place and returned to tell the tale, the mechanics assumed that that spot was *not* vulnerable to antiaircraft fire; additional armor was placed somewhere else on the fuselage. If a portion was undamaged, it probably was a vulnerable place.

Formula for Success

In order to start in the risk-measurement direction, management needs proven methods and tools. Management will succeed in this endeavor by:

- finding an easy-to-use and understandable methodology for measuring credit, market, and operational risks
- using historic and external loss data to forecast expected and unexpected losses

This chapter provides a bank executive with practical ways in which to measure and to successfully communicate risks to the bank. The measures presented for credit, market, and operational risk are simpler than those illustrated in Basel II yet assist a bank executive in obtaining an objective gauge of bank risks.

WHY MEASURE RISK?

Increased pressure from regulatory agencies to adopt more sophisticated risk measurement and management practices appears to be the tail wagging the dog: banks might not accept measurement complexity unless forced to do so. However, the tail that is wagging the regulatory dog is the more sophisticated practices themselves. Banks that do not move into the 21st century of risk quantification will be left behind.

MEASURING RISKS

The science behind risk measurement is relatively mature. The trouble (or perceived trouble) with risk measurement is that the metrics involved take a more than an average knowledge of statistical methods, standard distributions, and stochastic calculus. Further, some risks are hard to quantify.

This perceived complexity together with the degree of difficulty of quantification for some risks have led to the development of simpler frameworks, the most popular of which is the COSO framework from the 2004 Committee of Sponsoring Organizations (COSO) of the Treadway Commission. The COSO framework appears to be becoming the *de facto* standard for ERM.[72] While it provides a bank executive with a subjective assessment of risks in the enterprise, it falls short of establishing the single measure of risk that economic capital does.

As discussed in chapter 5, VAR is widely believed to be one of the best ways to measure a bank's market risk.[73] Most of the other measures for risk, no matter what the type, find their genesis in VAR. A VAR measurement describes the maximum likely loss a bank will experience in a given time period.[74] By determining how much of, and over what time period, a loss the bank can experience, management can readily identify its tolerances and appetite for the risks that it manages.

Statistical texts[75] provide a detailed explanation of probability theory using standard equations as VAR methodology. Although it is not exactly new science (it dates back to the early 1950s),[76] VAR has been more recently adapted for the derivation of a standard and simple-to-understand risk metric. Whereas the COSO framework gives management a subjective "feel" of the various risks in the company (one based largely on internal controls), VAR provides a number.

There is much debate about granularity; that is, to what degree of confidence should a bank go in calculating losses? Basel II banks will have to calculate their confidence levels at 99.9 percent, thereby significantly raising the amounts of capital set aside for unexpected loss. Since VAR has its limitations (it requires a large amount of historical data), the non-Basel II banks can use less intensive measures when managing risks and still determine a meaningful perspective on integrated risk management across all business units and portfolios in the bank.

Most important for determining strategy is developing economic capital, which is covered in depth in the next chapter. Two measures are integral to determining an economic capital figure: expected loss and unexpected loss (see chapter 6).

The rest of this chapter is devoted to assisting management with finding simple measures for expected and unexpected losses.

MEASURING MARKET RISK

By measuring market risk, a bank executive can manage it better. Management must be aware that the quality of any measurement is contingent on the broader enterprise risk management context in which the measurement itself takes place.[77] What happens to the bank's various portfolios when interest rates change? If the bank's portfolio contained only one asset, the value of the portfolio when interest rates change could be estimated by the asset's VAR, specifically by its duration. Since banks do not enjoy such simplicity, duration is not an accurate measure of market risk for a diversified portfolio.[78] However, since a plethora of external measures are available to correlate to the bank's internal ones, VAR works well in measuring expected and unexpected losses.

Before the VAR model, there were several tools that still have merit in assisting with measuring market risk: gap analysis, scenario analysis, and portfolio theory.[79] Scenario analysis was discussed in chapter 6. A brief discussion of the others follows.

Gap Analysis

Gap analysis is simply a "blunt instrument" in measuring interest-rate-risk exposure. Once a time horizon is selected, just as in VAR, management decides how much of the asset (or liability) portfolio will be repriced during the period. Then, management calculates interest-rate risk as follows:

$$\Delta NII = (GAP) \Delta r$$

where,

ΔNII = the change in net interest income

GAP = the difference between the asset portfolio amount and the liability portfolio amount repriced during the period

Δr = the change in interest rates

Portfolio Theory

Assuming that investors choose between portfolios for their return and the variance (or risk) in the return, applied to market risk, the same calculation (above) holds true. Like an investor, bank management will choose a portfolio based on its preferences for risk levels and expected return.

Measuring Operational (Event) Risk

Ascribing VAR to an operational loss event gets more complicated and exposes the limitations of VAR in calculating unexpected loss. After all, either one experiences a loss event (100% confidence) or does not (0% confidence). It is an either/or situation.

Take for example, a 99.9 percent safety record for an airline. Stated in VAR terms, this might mean that under current maintenance and weather conditions plus the training level of the crew, 999 planes out of 1,000 will not experience a loss (i.e., a crash). That may be of some assurance to the passengers of 999 of the planes, but not to those of the one loss.[80]

Consequently, we use the following equation to calculate an expected loss:[81]

$$\text{Expected loss (VAR)} = PE \times LGE$$

where,

PE = probability of event

LGE = loss, given the event

Since a loss is an either/or situation (a binomial distribution), the standard deviation is expressed:

$$\text{Standard deviation} = \sqrt{PE \times (1-PE)}$$

To calculate the amount of unexpected loss for this loss distribution, we apply the standard deviation to the loss, given the event (LGE):

$$\text{Unexpected Loss} = \sqrt{PE \times (1-PE)} \times LGE$$

Using our airline example, the expected loss of a $60 million aircraft, the LGE is: (1 − 99.9%) × $60 million = $60,000, which would be equal to the accounting-based loss provision of the airline. The unexpected loss and, therefore, the amount of economic capital set-aside is:

$$\text{Unexpected Loss} = \sqrt{99.9\% \times (1-99.9\%)} \times \$60 \text{ Million}$$

$$= \$1,896,418$$

MEASURING CREDIT RISK

The same calculations can be used to measure the economic capital for credit, using the concepts discussed in chapter 5, which adds one other element: exposure at default (EAD).

$$\text{Expected loss (loan loss provision)} = PD \times LGD \times EAD$$

where,

PD = probability of default

LGD = loss, given default

EAD = exposure at default

The unexpected loss, or economic capital, is calculated:

$$\text{Unexpected Loss (Economic Capital)} = \sqrt{PE \times (1-PD) \times LGE \times EAD}$$

A word of caution: The binomial equations described above tend to underestimate unexpected loss (and are certainly not Basel II compliant), but they can be used in comparing the degrees of risks in different portfolios and transactions. As with all measures of risk, these are never assumed to be the definitive "turnkey" decision-making tools. They inform critical thinking but should never be a substitution for it. The judgment of management, as always, is paramount.

CONCLUSION

Although VAR and its variants give the decision maker an educated guess about the risks the bank faces, it is never viewed as a "substitute for good management, experience, and judgment."[82] Having said that, the benefits of implementing economic capital systems are abundantly clear: risk-based pricing, risk-adjusted profitability measurement, improved strategic planning, and increased shareholder value (more on this in the next chapter).

Key Points

Measuring Banking Risk

- There are many tools the bank executive can use to measure credit, market, and operational risks. Different tools achieve different objectives. What is important in any evaluation of risk is a risk metric, a simple number, with which to properly communicate the level of risk in any endeavor.
- Risk measures range in complexity. The simplified tools presented in this chapter will form a basis for measuring risks and communicating them to management and employees.

Chapter 8

ECONOMIC CAPITAL AND DECISION MAKING

... tackle the question of how human beings recognize and respond to the probabilities they confront. This, ultimately, is what risk management and decision making are all about and where the balance between measurement and gut become the focal point of the whole story.

Peter L. Bernstein, economist and author,
from *Against the Gods: The Remarkable Story of Risk*

More than required, less than necessary. Those words sum up a tragic discovery made in the aftermath of the most infamous of naval disasters, the sinking of the Titanic.

For its 1912 maiden and only voyage, the Titanic carried 2,201 passengers. There were enough lifeboats for only 1,176 passagners. Curiously, the Titanic was "well capitalized" for its size; it was required only to have lifeboat capacity for 980. History, of course, tells us that this was not nearly enough.

Formula for Success

Regulatory capital cannot be the sole measure of safety and soundness. The bank executive has to measure the risks of the business and adjust the capital set-aside for them accordingly. Consequently, management will be sucessful if it:

- learns to measure appropriately the risks the bank faces
- manages bank risk in accordance with accepted tolerances
- uses risk measurement to enhance good judgment and sound decision making

In this chapter, we will discuss the principles of how economic capital and RAROC are used to measure risk, capital, and shareholder value in a framework that allows company-wide performance evaluation.

TOOLSS FOR CAPITAL ALLOCATION

In recent history, regulatory risk-based capital adequacy standards led banks and financial institutions to contemplate how each business line provided returns on equity. This brought about the determination of an equity-to-assets (or leverage) ratio for each line of business the bank provided. That framework views equity as a buffer against unexpected loss.[83]

The leverage ratio is simple and clear-cut. It provides banks and regulatory agencies with the amount of capital banks need to hold as a percentage of their assets. More advanced measures, however, such as those found in Basel II, are leading regulatory agencies to view the leverage ratio as an obsolete requirement for insurance against unexpected loss.[84] Change is inevitable, and the more sophisticated measures are expected to encourage banks to move to a disciplined alignment of "regulatory capital requirements with underlying risk profiles."[85]

From a regulatory and a shareholder perspective, banks not applying risk metrics, modeling, and economic capital analysis are exhibiting management deficiencies. Further, the excuses not to move to more sophisticated methodology are becoming slimmer: the costs of effective risk management and capital-allocation models no longer limit applying these models to the largest and most profitable banks. Many models are available, and their price continues to decline. Banks now can purchase the software and acquire a small staff of risk analysts (as apposed to credit analysts or financial analysts—it is a different skill set) to validate and interpret the models. Nevertheless, which model a bank elects to purchase depends on the complexity of its products as well as on internal resources and budget. Furthermore, because new models are introduced frequently, and given the complexity of some of these models, management should consult with their regulators, industry groups such as the Risk Management Association, and peer institutions for guidance about the most suitable model(s) for the bank.

Economic Capital

Over the past decade, the banking industry has accepted the term "economic capital" to describe the measure of risk in a bank, line of business, or portfolio and use the term "risk-adjusted return on capital" (RAROC) to note risk's link to capital. Many of the nation's leading and most profitable banks employ economic capital and RAROC analyses to manage their businesses. Banks that do not employ economic capital analytics suffer from inadequate insight into the risk and profitability of their businesses. They also are unable to compete with larger and often more sophisticated competitors.

Value Creation

Perhaps the most common pitfall banks (and banking analysts) make today is to measure performance solely against financial metrics, such as return on assets, return on equity, market share, and earnings growth. Though they are important performance ratios, they do not measure the creation of value. As a result, many financial institutions are developing economic capital and risk-adjusted performance measures to determine how much capital is necessary to support a line of business. They are measuring risk and return to calculate risk-adjusted profitability.

Increasingly, rating agencies recognize the importance of risk-based capital measures. Though regulatory capital adequacy is only one of several criteria that the agencies take into account when assigning a rating, analysts are finding that an enterprise-wide economic capital framework also is an important indicator of financial strength, good management strength, and board oversight.

Equity analysts, on the other hand, have long used economic capital and RAROC to understand the risk-adjusted profitability of the banks they analyze. Like equity analysts, more senior managers are using economic capital to compare risk-adjusted profitability across all lines of business.

For management, developing and implementing risk-assessment methodologies often presents a significant and difficult change in a bank's overall financial management philosophy and practices. Perhaps the single most important use of economic capital and RAROC is in directing strategic decisions about growing, shrinking, or fixing various lines of businesses, portfolios, or transactions within the bank. As a result, well-managed banks are integrating economic capital and RAROC into their strategic-planning processes.

Economic Capital versus Regulatory Capital

Economic capital is distinct from accounting or regulatory capital measures. It is the common language used to articulate levels of risk, profitability, and economic value. Most often, it is applied to credit, market, and operational risks.

The accounting view of capital is the most well-known. In general, the accounting definition of capital is the sum of items, such as the book value of shareholders equity, paid-in capital, and retained earnings. In this definition, capital is seen as a source of funding; risk is not reflected.

Defining regulatory capital is easy; it is the amount of capital the bank's regulators require. Like accounting capital, regulatory capital refers to specific categories of equity. However, regulators have defined "tiers" of capital in order to indicate various liquidity characteristics and capacities to absorb losses. In particular, regulators define an asset's loss potential by assigning the asset into various risk categories and then summing the balances within all weighting categories to derive "risk-weighted" assets. A bank's regulatory capital strength is measured in ratios, such as "Tier-1" capital to risk-weighted assets.

Economic capital differs significantly from both regulatory and accounting capital. It focuses largely on risk and is not based on accounting measures, funding strategy, or balance-sheet composition. Definitions of economic capital, however, vary. Relative to financial and regulatory capital, economic capital is the amount of equity capital necessary to cover potential losses, at a specific risk level, over a specific period of time.

Perhaps the most straightforward definition of economic capital was developed by Erisk, a global risk consulting firm. Economic capital "is a measure of risk in terms of economic realities, not regulatory or accounting rules, and is called economic capital because part of the measurement process involves converting a risk distribution to the amount of capital that is required to support the risk, in line with the institution's target financial strength (for example, credit rating)."[86]

Clearly this definition is a bit more esoteric than that of regulatory capital. However, the promises of economic capital management are far more valuable.

Economic capital is not an accounting measure; it is a risk measure that reflects the economic realities of the bank and individual lines of business within the bank. For example, how can management compare the relative riskiness of two unrelated functions, such as a data processing function and a lending function? Management needs only to calculate the economic capital for both processes in order to make an apples-to-apples comparison. Therefore, economic capital is a standardized measurement that can be used to compare different types of risk.

Finally, because it is a risk measure, it is therefore forward looking and considers changes in fair-market values (economic values) as opposed to accounting measures such as coupon rates or income streams. For these reasons, economic capital may be thought of as the "true" capital required to run the bank.

ECONOMIC CAPITAL AS A DECISION-MAKING TOOL

Economic capital models estimate the amount of capital needed to support the myriad risks throughout organization.

There are several key components of economic capital: expected loss, unexpected loss, hurdle rates, RAROC, and shareholder value-added (SVA).

Expected Loss

Expected loss, as discussed previously, is the average anticipated loss of a particular activity or transaction over time. These are the losses management expects to occur and are the price of admission to operate in the banking industry. They might include "benign" losses, such as daily teller outages, entry errors, and more serious losses due to internal and external fraud, charge-offs, and losses due to lawsuits.

Unexpected Loss

It should be fairly evident that expected losses do not tell the entire risk story. Anticipated losses are something that can be charged to operating expenses, mitigated by insurance, or controlled by internal policies, procedures, and limits. What about unexpected losses?

Unexpected loss is defined as the *potential for actual loss to exceed the expected loss and is a measure of the uncertainty inherent in the loss estimate.*[87] Unexpected loss is what makes the holding of capital necessary. Since economic capital is focused on maintaining enough capital to cover unexpected losses resulting from the risks the bank assumes, it can be expressed as protection against unexpected losses at a certain confidence level over a specific time horizon. (See chapter 5 for a discussion of the mathematical explanations of confidence levels and value-at-risk, or VAR.)

Hurdle Rates

Economic capital figures can be multiplied by a bank's hurdle rate to offer a RAROC number that is comparable across all lines of business within the bank. The hurdle rate is the minimum acceptable rate of return on the entire enterprise's equity,[88] or the enterprise-wide cost of capital.[89]

For example, a bank is considering several new lines of business (or product, service, portfolio, acquisition, and so forth). Traditional measures, such as return on equity—net income divided by equity—indicate the bank should invest in Line of Business D, or if the bank's hurdle rate (return on equity, ROE) is 10 percent, any of the lines of business except E are acceptable investments, as illustrated in exhibit 8.1.

RAROC

The output of various economic capital models also differs from other financial measures of capital adequacy. Model results are expressed as a dollar of capital necessary to adequately and profitably support the specific risk being assessed. Whereas most traditional measures of capital adequacy compare existing capital levels to assets, economic capital relates capital to risks, regardless of the existence of assets. Economic capital is based on an assessment of potential losses and is, therefore, a more forward-looking measure of capital adequacy than traditional accounting measures. The development and implementation of a well-functioning economic capital model

Exhibit 8.1 Sample Return on Equity Measures for Lines of Business

Line of Business	Return on Equity
A	14%
B	10%
C	12%
D	15%
E	8%

can therefore make bank management better equipped to anticipate and manage potential problems.

Defined as a ratio of risk-adjusted return to economic capital, RAROC is, in fact, a profitability measurement management and other stakeholders use to measure risk-adjusted performance and to provide a consistent view of economic profitability across all businesses units.

The following equation can be used to calculate RAROC:

$$\text{RAROC} = \frac{(\text{Net Income} - \text{Expected Losses})}{\text{Economic Capital Allocation}}$$

Shareholder Value-Added (SVA)

Finally, shareholder value-added (SVA), also known as "economic profit," is a dollar measure of performance. Shareholder value is created when earnings on capital are greater than the minimum required by investors (which is more than the minimum regulatory requirement) to compensate for risk over the investment period.[90] It is noted:

$$\text{SVA} = (\text{net income} - \text{expected losses}) - (\text{economic capital allocations} \times \text{hurdle rate})$$

Given the risk of the lines of business as illustrated above, changing the hurdle rate to a return on economic capital figure and exploring and defining the risks of new businesses with net income, expected loss, and economic capital allocations, the bank executive can compare risk return and value creation from one business line to the next (see exhibit 8.2). Here, both lines of business A and C are acceptable. They meet not only the bank's required RAROC hurdle but also the return on equity hurdle illustrated in exhibit 8.1.

An economic capital model therefore enables a more sophisticated, risk-based measure that ultimately will enhance shareholder value.

EXHIBIT 8.2   RAROC Comparison

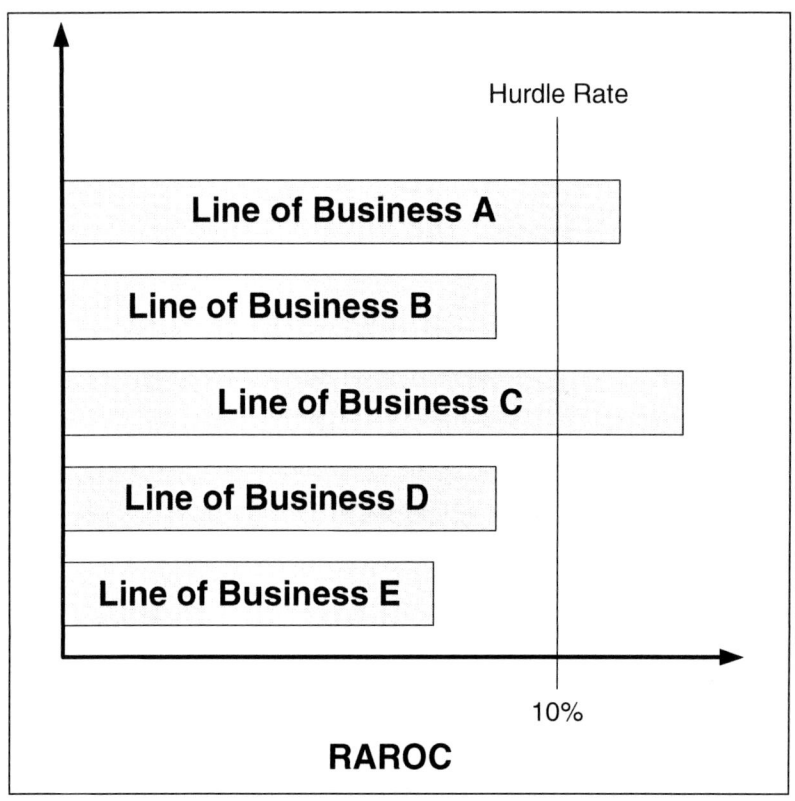

CONCLUSION

The benefits of implementing economic capital systems are abundantly clear: risk-based pricing, risk-adjusted profitability measurement, improved strategic planning, and increased shareholder value.

Recent changes in the banking industry continue to drive innovations in risk taking, performance measurement, and creating economic value. Value and risk-adjusted returns should be our buzz words, not just return on assets, return on equity, market share, and so forth, and managers must manage their banks for economic value, not for financial ratios.

Risk management programs must be aligned with shareholder interests. Because the essence of banking is risk taking, there's no point in developing robust profitability models that do not take risk into account.

Finally, managers and directors should consider that if they employ economic capital analysis to improve returns without taking on excessive risks, they inevitably will drive the bank's share price higher. Nevertheless, for banks that choose to wait, they too will be compelled by either the regulators or the market to adopt an economic capital model, but it will unfortunately be as a defensive move to forestall regulatory actions or loss of shareholder confidence rather than to drive shareholder value.

Key Points

Economic Capital and Decision Making

- ► Risk management programs must be aligned with shareholder interests.
- ► Recent changes in the banking industry continue to drive innovations in risk taking, performance measurement, and creating economic value.
- ► Economic capital allocation and RAROC are essential tools in assisting the bank executive with key decision making.

APPENDICES

Appendix A
ERM JOB DESCRIPTIONS

CRO JOB DESCRIPTION

XYZ Bank
Sample Position Description

Job Title: EVP/Chief Risk Officer
Department: Risk Management
Reports to: Board of Directors and CEO

Summary

The chief risk officer (CRO) will establish and manage an enterprise-wide risk management program. The CRO will assess all significant risks and exposures to the company's business lines and report on them to the bank's senior management and the board of directors. The CRO also will propose and implement recommendations to improve reporting systems, data integrity, and processes to identify, assess, and mitigate risks in all lines of business.

Essential Duties and Responsibilities

- ► Responsible for evaluating and enhancing the bank's business-line reports to measure and mitigate risks (i.e., credit risk, market risk, operational risk, compliance risk, interest rate risk, and so forth) and manage capital.
- ► Provide risk/reward and value-added analysis of all significant reports the business lines produce.

- Responsible for oversight of all credit scoring/grading reporting and migration models to monitor and measure credit risk and volatility.
- Responsible for evaluating the bank's aggregate credit exposure levels to individual counter-parties, industries, and so forth
- Responsible for the bank's allowance for loan and lease loss methodology and chairing the ALLL committee.
- Coordinate and implement as appropriate Basel II related risk-assessment processes.
- Responsible for implementing and reporting operational risk-tracking systems for key risk indicators, loss data, and so forth.
- Responsible for enhancing and managing the bank's compliance (regulatory risk) program.
- Responsible for presenting significant risk information to management with both strategic and tactical recommendations and action plans.
- Interact with bank regulators to provide insight into the bank's overall risk profile.
- Exercises the usual authority of a division manager concerning staffing, performance appraisals, promotions, salary recommendations, terminations, and budgets.

Supervisory Responsibilities

Manage a staff of risk reporting managers and analysts to ensure optimal performance in meeting the risk management division's goals and the objectives of the bank.

Personally initiate formal and informal communication and, at times, special projects, at appropriate levels both within and outside of the risk management division. Must also act as a consultant to the board of directors, senior management, and lines-of-business staff at all levels.

Develop technical and leadership skills for all team members while customizing education needs for individuals within the career-development framework. Retain the highest caliber professional staff while minimizing turnover. Aggressively prepare all levels of staff for future opportunities by identifying challenging work assignments, mentoring, and education programs to give employees exposure to proactive enterprise-wide problem solving. Recruit talented, motivated individuals to the bank as well as to the risk management division. Demonstrate personal development through mastery of the bank's leadership and education initiatives.

Qualifications
To perform this job successfully, an individual must be able to perform each duty satisfactorily. The requirements listed below are representative of the knowledge, skill, and/or ability required. Reasonable accommodations may be made to enable individuals with disabilities to perform the essential functions. Will direct and manage credit risk assessments outsourced to other companies.

Education and/or Experience
Undergraduate degree in economics, mathematics, statistics or related field required. Graduate degree or commensurate regulatory experience also is required. Must have at least 15 years of risk management experience, preferably in a regulatory or banking environment. Must be experienced in bank administration and have extensive knowledge of lending, operations, regulations, audit, compliance, treasury management, bank operations, Basel, Sarbanes-Oxley, and FDICIA. Significant regulatory experience is preferred.

Mathematical Skills
A strong background in mathematics and/or statistics is essential. Must be able to summarize and communicate analytical data commensurate with responsibilities.

Reasoning Ability
Must be able to analyze, evaluate, and solve practical problems and deal with a variety of concrete variables in situations where only limited standardization exists. Ability to interpret a

variety of instructions furnished in written, oral, diagram, or schedule form. Must also possess the ability to rationalize, think, and communicate at a conceptual level.

Computer Skills
Must be proficient in MS Windows and MS Office. Must possess the desire and ability to learn automated data-analysis tools and techniques.

Certificates, Licenses, Registrations
Graduate degree or commensurate regulatory experience and certifications are required.

Other Skills and Abilities
Must possess exceptional oral and written communications skills in order to communicate the company's overall risk profile in a simple and concise manner to managers, senior management, directors, and bank regulators.

Other Qualifications
Must possess strong consensus-building abilities. Must also be able to lead large, complex working groups.

Director, Credit Risk—Job Description

XYZ Bank
Sample Position Description

Job Title: SVP Commercial Credit Risk
Department: Commercial Credit Risk
Reports to: Chief Risk Officer

Summary

Assist in planning, developing, and implementing the risk management division's credit-risk framework. Develop and maintain the corporate commercial and retail credit-risk policies and guidelines and implement the division's credit-risk program. This framework will include business process analysis, a self-assessment program, and developing and monitoring key risk indicators (KRIs). Additional responsibilities include measuring losses and exposures, conducting root cause analysis, and driving change where necessary.

Responsible for evaluating commercial and retail credits. Direct the continuous independent and objective evaluation of underlying asset quality enterprise-wide. Maintain a risk-based review and analysis schedule for all affiliates, to ensure that an ongoing evaluation of the affiliates and/or products lines is completed and that emerging risks are identified in a timely fashion.

Display the ability to delegate work and communicate the risk management division's requirements to a diverse staff of executives, managers, and directors. Publish quarterly reports of key credit risk indicators at the enterprise, line-of-business, and product levels. Also responsible for participating in the achievement of corporate sales and service goals to build customer (external/internal) relationships and enhance shareholder value.

Essential Duties and Responsibilities include the following. Other duties may be assigned.

- Liaise with the bank's chief credit officer, lending staff, auditors, and other risk managers to establish an enterprise-wide framework that makes credit risks transparent, easily understood, and quantified on a timely basis so risks can be managed to realize maximum potential shareholder value.
- Liaise with executive officers, managers, auditors, bank regulators, and strategic planning committees to develop both qualitative and quantitative measures of credit risk.
- Ensure that credit risk measurement (Basel) and control processes (COSO) enterprise-wide are consistent with risk management's enterprise-wide objectives.
- Ensure that the credit risk staff is not just viewed as credit technicians, auditors, or policemen, but as business partners and leaders.
- Integrate the unit's credit risk assessments into risk management's economic capital model to allocate capital to business units in relation to risk exposures.
- Assist in developing and maintaining the company's loan loss reserve model.
- Keep informed of new developments and ideas, which would affect the company, by visiting other companies and banks, attending various association meetings, and interviewing vendors.
- Exercise management authority over staffing, performance appraisals, promotions, salary recommendations, and terminations.
- Perform other duties that periodically may be assigned.

Supervisory Responsibilities

Develop, measure, and periodically report performance measurements for credit risk review staff. Conduct at least annual performance evaluations of staff that identify specific strengths as well as areas of development. Actively recruit for any open positions in the department.

Personally initiate formal and informal communication and, at times, special projects at appropriate levels both within and outside of the risk management division. Act as a consultant to the chief credit officer and lending staff. Direct and manage credit risk assessments outsourced to other companies, consultants, or vendors.

Qualifications

To perform this job successfully, an individual must be able to perform each essential duty satisfactorily. The requirements listed below are representative of the knowledge, skill, and/or ability required. Reasonable accommodations may be made to enable individuals with disabilities to perform the essential functions.

Education and/or Experience

Undergraduate degree in business-related field required. MBA or commensurate regulatory certification is a plus. Must have at least 10 years of commercial credit assessment experience in a banking or a regulatory environment. Must be familiar with loan operations and Basel. Supervisory experience preferred.

Mathematical Skills

A strong background in mathematics and/or statistics is essential.

Reasoning Ability

This position requires a strong ability to rationalize and communicate at a conceptual level. Must be able to take theoretical concepts and apply them in an effective and practical manner.

Computer Skills

Must be proficient in MS Windows and MS Office. Must possess the desire and ability to learn computer modeling as well as other automated data-analysis tools and techniques.

Certificates, Licenses, Registrations

Risk management certifications are a plus; however, no special licenses or other certifications are required.

Other Skills and Abilities
Must possess exceptional oral and written communications skills, in order to communicate very detailed and very technical processes in a very simple and concise manner.

Other Qualifications
Must possess strong consensus-building abilities. Must be able to lead large, complex, multi-affiliate working groups.

Director, Market/Interest Rate Risk—Job Description

XYZ Bank
Sample Position Description

Job Title: SVP/Market Risk
Department: Market/Interest Rate Risk
Reports to: Chief Risk Officer

Summary

Lead the planning, development, and implementation of the risk management division's market-risk framework. This framework will include evaluating Treasury function processes, developing and monitoring key risk indicators (KRIs) used for assessing interest rate sensitivity and liquidity, and identifying emerging risks. As necessary, propose and implement recommendations to improve reporting systems, data integrity, and processes to identify, assess, and mitigate market risk.

Be able to delegate work and communicate the risk management division's requirements to a diverse staff of executives, managers, and directors. Publish quarterly reports of key credit-risk indicators at the enterprise, line-of-business, and product levels. Participate in achieving corporate sales and service goals to build customer (external/internal) relationships and enhance shareholder value.

Essential Duties and Responsibilities

- Responsible for evaluating and enhancing risk monitoring and reporting solutions to measure and mitigate market risks and preserve capital.
- Provide risk/reward and value-added analysis of all significant reporting produced by the Treasury function. Items considered in the review include the:
    1. appropriateness of the risk-measurement systems given the nature, scope, and complexity of the bank's activities
    2. accuracy and completeness of data inputs

3. reasonableness and validity of scenarios and assumptions
4. validity of the risk-measurement calculations
- Responsible for presenting significant risk information to management with both strategic and tactical recommendations and action plans.
- Interface with regulators to provide insight into the bank's market/interest-rate risk profile.
- Liaise with the bank's asset liability management staff and auditors to establish an enterprise-wide framework that makes market risks transparent and easily understood and quantified on a timely basis so risks can be managed to realize maximum potential shareholder value.
- Liaise with executive officers, managers, auditors, bank regulators, and strategic planning committees to develop quantitative measures of market risk.
- Ensure that market-risk measurement and control processes in affiliates as well as Treasury function units are consistent with risk management's enterprise-wide objectives.
- Ensure that the market-risk management is not just viewed as technicians or policemen, but as a business partner by the line operating managers.
- Integrate market risk assessment into risk management's risk-adjusted economic capital model to allocate capital to business units in relation to risk exposures.
- Keep informed of new developments and ideas that could affect the company by visiting other companies and banks, attending various association meetings, and interviewing vendors.
- Perform other duties as periodically may be assigned.

Supervisory Responsibilities

Personally initiate formal and informal communications and special projects at appropriate levels within and outside the risk management division. Consult with asset/liability management team, the ALCO, the board of directors, senior management, and risk management staff at all levels. Actively recruit for any open positions in the department.

Qualifications
To perform this job successfully, an individual must be able to carry out each essential duty satisfactorily. The requirements listed below are representative of the knowledge, skill, and/or ability required.

Education and/or Experience
Undergraduate degree in business-related field required. Graduate degree or commensurate regulatory experience is a plus. Must have at least 10 years of market/interest-rate risk assessment experience, preferably in a regulatory or banking environment. Must be experienced in Treasury operations and Basel. Significant supervisory experience preferred.

Mathematical Skills
A strong background in mathematics and/or statistics is essential. Must be able to summarize and communicate analytical data commensurate with responsibilities.

Reasoning Ability
Because it is largely analytical, this position requires a strong ability to rationalize, think, and communicate at a conceptual level.

Computer Skills
Must be proficient in MS Windows and MS Office. Must possess the desire and ability to learn automated data-analysis tools and techniques, including simulation modeling, stress testing, and pricing.

Certificates, Licenses, Registrations
Graduate degree or commensurate regulatory experience and certifications.

Other Skills and Abilities
Must possess exceptional oral and written communications skills in order to communicate the company's overall risk profile in a very simple and concise manner to managers, senior management, directors, and bank regulators.

Other Qualifications
Must possess strong consensus-building abilities. Must be able to lead large, complex working groups.

Director, Operational Risk—Job Description

XYZ Bank
Sample Position Description

Job Title: SVP, Operations Risk
Department: Operational Risk
Reports to: Chief Risk Officer

Summary

Assist in planning, developing, and implementing the risk management division's operational risk framework. This framework will include business process analysis, a self-assessment program, development of key risk indicators (KRIs) and service standards for the each affiliate's lines of business. Additional responsibilities will be to measure losses and exposures, conduct root cause analysis, and drive change where necessary. Lead the company in establishing a framework for understanding, identifying, measuring, and mitigating operating risks across the enterprise. Provide decision support to executive management in managing operating risk. Responsible for participating in achieving corporate sales and service goals to build customer (external/internal) relationships and enhance shareholder value.

Essential Duties and Responsibilities

- ► Liaise with CFOs and auditors to establish an enterprise-wide framework that makes operating risks transparent and easily understood and quantified on a timely basis so risks can be managed to realize maximum potential shareholder value.
- ► Liaise with executive officers, managers, internal auditors, and strategic planning committees to develop quantitative measures of operational risk.
- ► Ensure that operating-risk measurement and control processes in affiliates as well as business units are consistent with risk management's enterprise-wide objectives.

- Develop and manage process to report and track operational loss experience in business units as well as for affiliates and the holding company as a whole.
- Integrate operational risk into risk management's risk-adjusted economic capital model to allocate capital to business units in relation to risk exposures.
- Direct the study and establishment of new and revised systems, procedures, methods, and forms that would be used in, or have an effect on, the operations activities at the holding company level as well as at the affiliate level.
- Keep informed of new developments and ideas that would affect the company, by visiting other companies and banks, attending various association meetings, and interviewing vendors.
- Exercise the usual authority of a manager concerning staffing, performance appraisals, promotions, salary recommendations, and terminations.
- Perform other duties as may be assigned.

Supervisory Responsibilities

Develop, measure, and periodically report performance measurements for operational risk staff. Conduct at least annual performance evaluations of staff that identify specific strengths as well as areas of development. Actively recruit for any open positions in the department.

Personally initiate formal and informal communication and initiate special projects at appropriate levels both within and outside the risk management division. Act as a consultant to the CFO, internal auditors, risk managers, and affiliate banks.

Qualifications

To perform this job successfully, an individual must be able to carry out each essential duty satisfactorily. The requirements listed below are representative of the knowledge, skill, and/or ability required. Reasonable accommodations may be made to enable individuals with disabilities to perform the essential functions.

Education and/or Experience
Undergraduate degree in business-related field required. MBA or commensurate certification is a plus. Must have at least eight years of business experience, preferably in a banking or auditing environment. Must have knowledge of bank operations, Basel, Sarbanes-Oxley, and FDICIA controls assessment process. Supervisory experience preferred.

Mathematical Skills
A strong background in mathematics and/or statistics is essential.

Reasoning Ability
Because it is largely analytical, this position requires a strong ability to rationalize and to think and communicate at a conceptual level. Must be able to take theoretical concepts and apply them in an effective and practical manner.

Computer Skills
Must be proficient in MS Windows and MS Office. Must possess the desire and ability to learn computer modeling as well as other automated data-analysis tools and techniques.

Certificates, Licenses, Registrations
Risk management certifications are a plus; however, no special licenses or other certifications are required.

Other Skills and Abilities
Must possess exceptional oral and written communications skills in order to communicate very detailed and very technical processes in a simple and concise manner.

Other Qualifications
Must possess strong consensus-building abilities. Must be able to lead large, complex, multi-affiliate working groups.

Physical Demands

The physical demands described here are representative of those that must be met by an employee to successfully perform the essential functions of this job. Reasonable accommodations may be made to enable individuals with disabilities to perform the essential functions.

Work Environment

The work environment characteristics described here are representative of those an employee encounters while performing the essential functions of this job. Reasonable accommodations may be made to enable individuals with disabilities to perform the essential functions.

Appendix B
RISK MANAGEMENT PLAN

OBJECTIVES IN THE RISK MANAGEMENT PLAN

The purpose of this plan is to provide a road map to managing risk. The root of this plan is a bank's risk management policy, which outlines some simple and pragmatic techniques for identifying, assessing, managing and reporting on the more prominent risks facing the company. This plan is based on the bank's current risk assessment and analysis. As the risk management function evolves, the plan will be revised as appropriate.

This plan focuses principally on credit risk, market risk, operational risk, regulatory risk, legal risk, reputation risk, and strategic risk. As other genres of risk are identified and increase in significance, they too will be incorporated into the bank's risk management plan.

The board of directors and senior management are responsible for understanding the company's risk management objectives and risk tolerance. Therefore, communication is fundamental to a successful partnership between the risk management division and bank managers and board members. Risk management must engage in active reporting and conversations with all managers, and within every line of business, to determine appropriate standards and measures.

This risk management plan will be monitored annually to ensure that it—and the techniques it stipulates for identifying, assessing, and managing risk—is achieving the desired results and that changes to the company's risk profile are reflected effectively.

Risk Management Policy

The policy, which defines risk and risk management, specifies the role of the Chief Risk Officer, the Risk Management Division, senior management, and the board. The policy also highlights risk concepts, identifies the most prevalent types of risk to the company, stipulates risk reporting, and points out the importance of continuous training and maintaining associations with other banking and risk professionals.

The Risk Management Procedures

The risk management procedures provide a framework for implementing the risk management policy. In short, the procedures specify that a qualitative risk assessment of credit, market, operational, regulatory, legal, reputation, and strategic risks will be conducted in the bank and its affiliates. The assessment will characterize risk levels as low, moderate, or high and risk trends as increasing, stable, or decreasing.

Appendix C
RISK MANAGEMENT POLICY

INTRODUCTION

There is no "best way" to perform risk management, although it is important to start out with a simple process in order to establish a solid operating framework. Developing a simple, yet solid, operating framework for risk management allows for increasing sophistication over time.

This policy focuses on the more fundamental components of a successful risk management program. Rather than place too much emphasis on sophisticated estimation models, more emphasis will be placed initially on important managerial and judgmental elements. These elements include the clarity of risk policies, the strength of internal controls, the degree of management discipline, the level of internal risk transparency, and, ultimately, the experience and market knowledge of risk managers.

Therefore, this policy sets out to outline simple and pragmatic techniques for identifying, assessing, and managing the more prominent risks facing a company.

DEFINITIONS

Risk

In fundamental terms, risk may be defined as a deviation from the expected, resulting in possible loss and erosion of real and economic capital.

Risk Management

Risk management is a process consisting of well-defined steps that, when taken in sequence, support better decision making by contributing to a greater insight into risks and their consequences. It is as much about identifying opportunities as it is about avoiding losses. By adopting effective risk management techniques, a company can improve its business performance.

Risk management as a centralized activity must accomplish the following tasks:

- identify concerns
- identify risks and risk owners
- evaluate risks as to likelihood and consequences
- assess options for accommodating the risks
- prioritize risk management efforts
- develop risk management plans
- authorize implementation of the risk management plans
- track risk management efforts and manage accordingly

RISK MANAGEMENT STRUCTURE

The basic structure for the risk management division consists of a chief risk officer and various risk managers who are responsible for the definition, structure, implementation, and coordination of a risk management approach consistent with the program approved by the company's board of directors.

The chief risk officer's job is to coordinate risk management activities within the company and with all its affiliates.

The chief risk officer schedules and oversees the production of all risk reviews, either as stand-alone events or as part of management reviews. This entails alerting risk owners and risk committee members of support requirements for such reviews.

The chief risk officer is responsible for:

- preparing and distributing the minutes from risk committee meetings

- coordinating and presenting a summary of risk management activities at all major reviews
- developing and implementing the risk management program
- identifying and assessing the experience and educational requirements for all risk management staff and consultants
- providing training in risk management
- coordinating risk management activities
- preparing reports and other briefing materials for senior management and the board

The Role of the Chief Risk Officer

The role of the chief risk officer is to develop and formalize risk management activities and results. This role includes being spokesperson about the company's risks.

The chief risk officer, an executive officer of the company, is responsible for drafting and implementing risk management policies and procedures. However, the chief risk officer does not have direct ownership of any risks per se.

The Role of Risk Managers

A risk manager's primary job is to assist in assessing, coordinating, and tracking the company's risk management activities and to perform the routine board and review functions. The risk manager provides a focus for risk assessment (re-review) for all business functions. Any new risks are captured in the ongoing process.

Risk Management Committee

A part of the company's risk management effort will be devoted to implementing a risk management committee consisting of managers and directors. These persons do not have to be risk owners, although they may be. This committee shall meet routinely to provide high-level visibility to the risk management process. The chief risk officer (chairman) and committee members shall discuss significant risk issues and present summaries of progress or nonprogress in managing those risks. The minutes of this meeting, including significant findings, will be documented in writing and presented to the company's CEO and board of directors.

Risk Concepts

The following are a few key concepts in managing risks:

- principles
- ownership
- management
- types of risk

Principles

There are no fundamental scientific laws in risk management akin to the laws of motion, conservation, and continuity from which applied scientific results are obtained. Much of risk management is qualitative and subject to judgment colored by experience and perspective. However, one fundamental principle can be postulated and used:

> *Any element of the company's business that entails a new venture or is not part of the core operating activities for the company is a source of risk.*

Risk management must become involved by identifying the risk aspects of the venture in question, and then in developing strategies to avoid, mitigate, or otherwise accommodate the issues identified, according to the company's risk appetite.

Ownership

The most important aspect of risk ownership is a clear mutual understanding of the risk and of the responsibilities of risk managers. The second most important aspect is for the company's board of directors to have a similar understanding of risks on an enterprise-wide basis.

Failure to understand and own risks can result in wrongly conceived priorities and failure in the risk management process. Therefore, every significant risk identified by the program should have an affiliate, department, and manager identified as the owner of that particular risk.

Management

Risk management is the process of assessing risk, taking steps to reduce risk to an acceptable level, maintaining that level of risk, and reporting risks to the bank's senior management and the board. To do this, risk management seeks to predict the probability of an event (default or otherwise), the time frame over which the event will occur, and the potential impact of the event.

Risk management also plans ways to respond to anticipated hazards as well as catastrophic events. It does this by applying a range of management techniques to identify, evaluate, treat, and monitor risk.

Types of Risks

While a complete list of all of the company's risks would be impossibly long, the more immediate and most significant (broadly defined) risks are credit, market, and operational (including regulatory, legal, reputation, and strategic).

Credit Risk Credit risk is generally defined as the risk due to uncertainty in a counter-party's ability to perform on a credit obligation. In assessing credit risk from a counter-party, the company must consider two issues:

1. *Credit quality:* This encompasses both the likelihood of the counter-party defaulting as well as possible recovery rates in the event of a default.
2. *Credit exposure:* In the event of a default, what is the replacement cost of the counter-party's outstanding obligations likely to be.

Market Risk Market risk is the possibility of financial loss caused by unfavorable movements in market variables. Typically, market risk at financial institutions is significantly influenced by:

- *Liquidity risk,* the risk that an investment, when converted to cash, will experience loss in its value.
- *Interest-rate risk,* the risk that the value of an asset or liability will change in response to a change in interest rates.
- *Inflation risk,* the danger that the dollars one invests will buy less in the future because prices of consumer goods rise. When the rate of inflation rises, investments have less purchasing power. This is especially true with investments that earn fixed rates of return. As long as they are held at constant rates, they are threatened by inflation.
- *Exchange-rate risk,* the chance that a nation's currency will lose value when exchanged for foreign currencies.
- *Reinvestment risk,* the danger that reinvested money will fetch returns lower than those earned before reinvestment. Individuals with dividend-reinvestment plans and bondholders are subject to this risk.

Operational Risk Operational risk is generally defined as the risk of loss caused by deficiencies in information systems, business processes, or internal controls as a result of either internal or external events.

Most operational risks are best managed within the departments in which they arise. Information technology professionals are best suited for addressing systems-related risks.

Back-office staff are best suited to address settlement risks, and so forth. However, a centralized operational risk management department should provide overall planning, coordination, and monitoring. This central department should coordinate closely with market risk and credit risk management departments within an overall enterprise risk management framework.

Operational risks include:

- *Legal risk:* Legal risk arises from the potential that changes in the law, unenforceable contracts, legal proceedings, or illegal or unethical conduct can disrupt or otherwise negatively affect the operations or condition of the bank.
- *Reputation risk:* Reputation risk is the current and prospective impact on earnings and capital arising from negative public opinion. This risk affects the institution's ability to establish new relationships or services or continue servicing existing relationships. It may expose the institution to litigation, financial loss, or a decline in its customer base. Reputation risk exposure, which is present throughout the organization, includes the responsibility to exercise caution in dealing with customers and the community.
- *Regulatory risk:* This risk associated with failing to comply with laws related to banking and related practices. The banking industry is one of the most heavily regulated, and, therefore, regulatory risk is one of the most significant areas of concern to any bank. Changes in banking laws create additional risks and may have a substantial impact on operations. Failure to comply with banking laws may result in heavy fines and penalties. Consumer compliance regulations, the Bank Secrecy Act, and the Community Reinvestment Act constitute some of the more significant, fundamental genres of regulations for any bank.
- *Strategic risk:* Strategic risk is the current and prospective impact on earnings or capital arising from adverse

business decisions, improper implementation of decisions, or lack of responsiveness to industry changes. This risk is a function of the compatibility of an organization's strategic goals, the business strategies developed to achieve the goals, the resources deployed to reach the goals, and the quality of implementation.

Risk Profile Report

Not to be confused with the risk management program, the risk profile report is an executive-level document summarizing risk management's perception of credit risk, operational risk, regulatory risk, market risk, legal risk, and reputation risk in terms of high, moderate, low and increasing, stable, or decreasing for each affiliate and the company as a whole.

Elements of risk will be assigned a risk rating (also termed level of risk) that is determined by combining estimates of likelihood and consequence in the context of any existing control measures.

The risk profile report should be published quarterly and presented to affiliate CEO's, their boards, and the senior managers of the holding company and its board.

Risk Management Tools

Some basic risk management tools are needed to assist in assessing risks, to ensure that risk assessments address all pertinent aspects of the program, and to provide a specific means of overcoming the underlying bases for the risks. Aside from basic office equipment and modeling tools, these tools include participation in professional organizations, maintenance of professional designations, subscriptions to appropriate journals and publications, training, and attendance at appropriate meetings and conferences.

Appendix D
RISK MANAGEMENT PROCEDURES

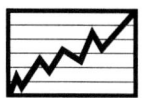

INTRODUCTION

The criteria used to assess risk are based primarily on the level and direction of risk and the potential consequences of risk. A good risk management program, therefore, should include procedures necessary to manage existing risks and ensure the timely detection of emerging risks.

Concerns versus Risks

A concern to be evaluated as a potential risk is literally any issue about which a doubt exists in some context. A procedure should be put in place for reviewing concerns and identifying those that actually engender risks. Some differentiation between concerns and risks needs to be made because complicated things, like some concerns, often get confused with risky things.

The best person in the bank to decide what are concerns and what are risks is the chief risk officer. In fact, making such distinctions is one of his major responsibilities: he alone should have the responsibility to declare formally that an issue is or is not a risk.

It is also necessary for the chief risk officer to allocate responsibility for resolving risks to the appropriate function, specialty, or discipline. Ultimately, senior management and the board bear the ownership of risk.

Evaluate Risks as to Consequences and Likelihood

For risk management, generally there is little precision in either the metric for the probability of occurrence of risk or the metric for the consequences of risk. Therefore, the level of risk expressed as a combination of possibility and consequences may suffice even if some pseudo-mathematical approaches are used.

Risk officers should use whatever tools are available and meaningful in a given situation, and they should not get hung up on mathematically appearing artifices that do not really have any more precision than an informed judgment.

Risk Management Options

Risk management options typically include avoidance, control, assumption, and risk transfer.

Avoidance: Use an alternate approach that does not have the risk. This mode is not always an option. There are functions and products that deliberately involve high risks in the expectation of high gains. However, if it can be applied, this is the most effective risk management technique.

Control: This involves developing a risk-reduction plan and then tracking to the plan. Control measures include managing product mix, growth, concentrations, regulatory compliance, internal controls, and audit.

Assumption: Simply accepting the risk and proceeding. A word of caution: there is often a tendency within financial organizations to gradually let the assumption of a risk take on the aura of a controlled risk.

Risk transfer: An attempt to pass the risk to a counterparty. Typical examples of methods used to transfer risk include hedges or swaps, pricing, participations or syndications, guarantees, and insurance.

Prioritize Risk Management Efforts

Once risks have been evaluated in terms of likelihood of occurrence and consequences, and when options for risk management have been reviewed, risk management must rank the risks and assign priorities. The chief risk officer ultimately is responsible for sorting all of the mechanical aspects of the risks (ranks and risk management options) and presenting them to the board as a complete package.

The board of directors must exercise its judgment to prioritize resources for risk management purposes. The ranked risks are reviewed in terms of combined likelihood and consequences and in terms of level of concerns with missions, functions, and business objectives.

Develop Risk Management Plans

The chief risk officer is responsible for developing a risk management program that addresses the most significant risks at the enterprise level, the affiliate level, and the program or line-of-business level.

Risk management will develop assessment schedules detailing the frequency and focus of its efforts to assess credit risk, market risk, operation risk, and regulatory risk. The depth, breadth, scope, and frequency of these assessments should be discussed with senior management and the board.

The program should encompass an approach to risk management that emphasizes that risks may be considered to be low, moderate, or high. Risks given a low ranking can be delegated to routine management; such risks typically do not require specific risk management plans.

Implementation of the Risk Management Plans

The chief risk officer is responsible for assessing, presenting, authorizing, and implementing the risk management program. The chief risk officer is responsible for presenting the status of the program to management and the board of directors, not less than quarterly.

Appendix E

ELEMENTS OF AN ENTERPRISE RISK MANAGEMENT COMMITTEE CHARTER

The ERM committee is responsible for risk management, internal compliance, and control systems. The committee should:

1. Establish and implement risk management and internal compliance and control systems, and ensure that a mechanism is in place for assessing the efficiency and effectiveness of those systems.
2. Approve and recommend to the board for adoption policies and procedures on risk oversight and management to establish an effective and efficient system for:
    a. identifying, assessing, monitoring, and managing risk
    b. disclosing any material changes to the bank's overall risk profile
3. Regularly review the bank's risk profile.
4. Assess the adequacy of the internal risk-control systems with management and auditors.
5. Monitor the effectiveness of the bank's internal-controls system.
6. Ensure that the risk management system considers all material risks, including risks arising from:
    a. implementing strategies (strategic risk)
    b. operations or external events (operational risk)
    c. legal and regulatory compliance (legal risk)
    d. changes in community expectation of corporate behavior (reputation risk)

e. a counterparty's financial obligations within a contract (credit risk)
   f. changes in financial and physical market prices (market risk)
   g. being unable to fund operations or convert assets into cash (liquidity risk)
7. Assess if management has controls in place for unusual transactions and any potential transactions that may carry more than an acceptable degree of risk.
8. Assess the prioritization of greatest potential financial risks, including:
   a. safeguarding assets
   b. litigation and claims
   c. noncompliance with laws, regulations, standards, and best practice guidelines that may result in significant financial loss
   d. important judgments and accounting estimates
   e. maintaining proper accounting records
9. Assess the internal processes for determining areas of greatest risks.
10. Report to the board on the adequacy of the risk management process.
11. Review risk reports from management, including reports of any actual or suspected fraud, theft, or suspicious activity.
12. Monitor compliance with legal and regulatory obligations.
13. Confirm that management has adopted a system of internal controls designed to ensure accurate and timely financial reporting.
14. Review management's processes for ensuring and monitoring compliance with laws, regulations, and other requirements relating to financial and nonfinancial reporting.
15. Review for completeness and accuracy management's reporting of corporate governance practices.

Appendix F

ENTERPRISE RISK MANAGEMENT ORGANIZATIONAL CHART

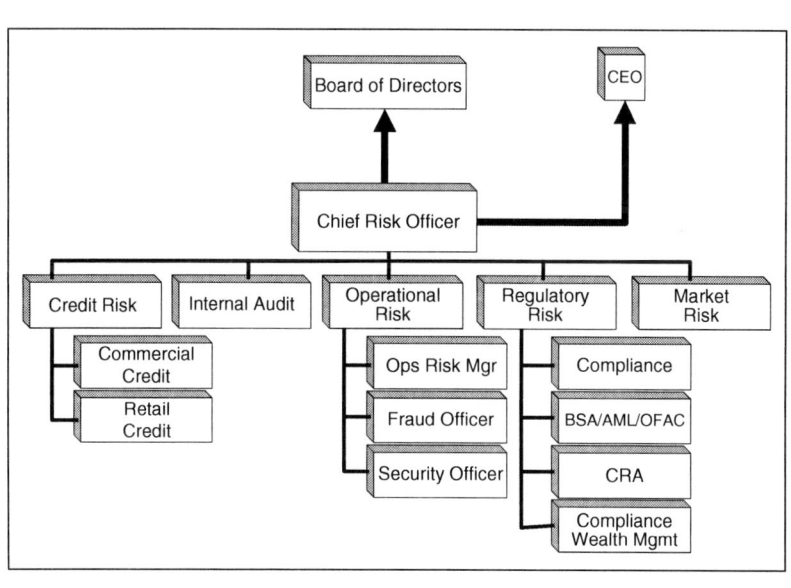

Appendix G
SAMPLE RISK PROFILE REPORT FOR THE BOARD OF DIRECTORS

ENTERPRISE RISK MANAGEMENT DIVISION
OCTOBER 15, 200X

FIRST CREDIT BANK
Current Risk Profile

	Previous Year		Current Year		
Risk Category	Sept 30	Dec 31	Mar 31	June 30	Sept 30
Commercial Credit Risk	Moderate/S	Moderate/S	Moderate/S	Moderate/I	Moderate/S
Retail Credit Risk	Moderate/S	Low/S	Low/S	Low/S	Low/S
Regulatory (Compliance) Risk	Moderate/S	Moderate/S	Moderate/S	Moderate/S	Moderate/S
Operational Risk	Moderate/S	Moderate/S	Low/S	Low/I	Low/I
Bank Secrecy Act	Moderate/S	Moderate/S	Low/S	Low/S	Low/S
Community Reinvestment Act	Low/S	Low/S	Low/S	Low/S	Low/S
Market Risk	Moderate/S	Moderate/S	Moderate/I	Moderate/I	Moderate/S
Legal Risk	Low/S	Low/S	Low/S	Low/S	Low/S
Reputation Risk	Not Rated	Not Rated	Low/S	Low/S	Low/S
Strategic Risk	Not Rated	Not Rated	Not Rated	Moderate/S	Moderate/S

Table denotes 'Risk Level/Direction', i.e. 'Low', 'Moderate', 'High' and 'Increasing' (I), 'Stable' (S), 'Decreasing' (D).

First Credit Bank's composite risk profile remains relatively unchanged from the previous quarter and is considered by the Risk Management Division to be "Moderate" and Stable (S).

This assessment is based on reviews conducted by the Risk Management Division as well as regulatory examination findings and conclusions drawn by the bank's internal and external auditors. Neither the level of risk nor the direction in risk trends is considered to be a significant concern. It is important to note that a preponderance of rating "Low/S" does not necessarily mean that the company's composite risk rating will also be "Low/S." In reality, not all risks are given equal weight. Therefore, the company's composite rating always will be biased in favor of those disciplines that have the most direct impact on earnings and capital.

CREDIT RISK

As of September 30, 200X, FCB reported classified assets totaling $26.7 million, representing a manageable 19.9 percent of Tier-1 capital and reserves. However, adjusting this total for additional credits downgraded by the Risk Management Division after the quarter, classified assets increased to approximately $30.3 million, exceeding the policy threshold of 30 percent of Tier-1 capital and reserves. The most significant commercial credits contributing to this increase include ABC Corp ($3.2 million), Oxford Enterprises, LLC ($1.2 million), and Bob's Super Burgers ($1.1 million).

The bank reported a slight decline in delinquencies (30–89 days) in the C&I and multifamily loan portfolios with no commercial credits delinquent in excess of 90 days. The overall level of delinquencies and nonaccruals in both the CRE and C&I portfolios is not considered a concern.

Commercial loan losses in both nonfarm/nonresidential CRE and C&I portfolios are comparable to those reported in the previous quarter and remain slightly in excess of peer medians. The bank continues to experience no losses in the multifamily portfolio. Given manageable levels of classified loans, nonaccruals, and loan losses, the bank's loan loss reserve ratio (LLR/Total Loans) of 1.45 percent is considered adequate.

Risk management downgraded an unacceptable 12.2 percent of the commercial credit relationships reviewed during the quarter, including seven double downgrades. Most of the downgrades occurred in commercial credits administered at the branch level. Similarly, the Risk Management Division found that loan files lacked or contained dated financial statements in 11 percent of the commercial credits reviewed. A majority of the documentation exceptions occurred in commercial credits administered at the branches. Nevertheless, management has made effective changes in tracking and obtaining loan documentation at the bank's main office.

Retail mortgage and installment loan delinquencies (30–89 days) remain significantly below levels reported last year. Total delinquency levels are considered good and compare very favorably to peer. Delinquencies and losses within the credit card portfolio continue to decline. Management's efforts to reduce retail loan delinquencies are proving to be effective.

Mortgage nonaccruals continue to decline but remain significantly in excess of peer medians. Nonaccruals within the retail installment loan portfolio have stabilized at levels significantly in excess of peer medians. Likewise, retail mortgage loan and installment loan losses remain significantly greater than peer. Management is urged to develop action plans designed to reduce nonaccruals and losses to more acceptable levels.

OPERATIONAL RISK

While the use of self-assessment questionnaires and operational loss matrices for each affiliate has been established in conjunction with the Sarbanes-Oxley documentation, the operational risk-assessment process is not yet fully functional. The Risk Management Division is working to identify and categorize losses as defined by the Basel Committee. Loss categorization is difficult in any company and is no different for this bank. Once identified and categorized, all similar loss types also must be tracked over a period of time. The Risk Management Division is meeting with other financial institutions and practitioner's groups to discuss "best-practice" solutions to these challenges.

Based on responses obtained from the operational risk self-assessments completed by management, as well as discussions with management at all levels of the corporation, no significant extraordinary operational losses have occurred through September 200X.

Furthermore, internal audits of the bank's financial statements and internal control systems have not uncovered any significant control weaknesses.

REGULATORY RISK

Senior management is becoming actively involved in managing the bank's regulatory risks, and issues raised by the Risk Management Division and the OCC are being addressed on a timelier basis.

The most significant item being monitored at this time is the possibility that the bank may need to reimburse some customers for fees charged on overdraft lines of credit. The regulation is not clear on this issue, so the Risk Management Division submitted a request to the Federal Reserve Board for definitive guidance. If the regulators determine that the fees must be counted as finance charges, the disclosures will be in violation of Regulation Z. The bank may need to reimburse consumers for these fees.

Also, the quality of the loan documentation received from auto dealers varies and, in some instances, includes technical violations of Reg. Z and potential violations of Reg. B. This has been discussed with management, who agreed to remind the bank's loan officers to document only those factors that relate directly to the credit underwriting decision.

BANK SECRECY ACT

The BSA officer has updated the bank's BSA/OFAC/Patriot Act policy and procedures and training materials. During the second and third quarters of 200X, the BSA officer conducted annual training.

A "Customer Identification Program" policy and procedure were implemented October 1, 200X, as required by the Patriot Act. BSA officers are monitoring the bank's compliance. New regulatory examination guidelines have been received and were discussed at the quarterly BSA officer meeting. Additional procedures are being developed to address the new regulatory requirements.

The BSA officers are reviewing anti-money laundering software vendors. During October 200X, BSA officers attended a technical presentation by Bankers System for the Atchley Anti-Money Laundering Solutions. A visit to a bank using this solution is scheduled for December 200X.

COMMUNITY REINVESTMENT ACT

The bank's CRA officer's analysis of the 200X CRA program indicated substantial improvement in making loans within the bank's assessment area.

In their most recent examination, OCC rated both the lending test and the service test as "Outstanding." The investment test was rated "High Satisfactory."

No significant issues with the bank's CRA program have been identified.

Market Risk

The bank continues to maintain a positive correlation of EVE changes to interest rate shock changes. The modeling results are within policy limits. The OCC canary report highlights that the depreciation of Tier-1 capital changed from −3.61 percent in 2003 to 8.15 percent as of June 30, 200X, due to the increasing rate environment.

Although considered a moderate risk, the OCC canary report shows an increase in most of the liquidity risk factors. The loan-to-deposit ratio dropped slightly, while the dependency ratio has improved since last quarter. Borrowings also have been reduced this quarter, partially due to the sale of loans.

Funding risk at First Credit Bank is considered "High" due to increased use of Federal Home Loan Bank borrowing capacity and reliance on brokered CDs. Currently, approximately 56 percent of the bank's FHLB borrowing lines have been drawn and $165 million remains available. The bank's management and ALCO committee are addressing this risk by aggressively originating deposits and by adjusting the bank's loan strategies, including loan sales.

The holding company and the bank are implementing a new ALM model, BancWare's convergence product. There exists the potential for erroneous results from either model due to invalid inputs, assumptions, and/or data errors.

Legal Risk

The volume of pending material legal proceedings, three cases, is low and manageable. Two of the three proceedings involve issues that present a low level of risk to the bank. The first case is threatened litigation involving a claim that the bank's trust department failed to send all its customers a Thanksgiving turkey. Should this case be filed, a favorable outcome is anticipated.

The second case is a lawsuit filed by First Credit Bank against Down Home Commerce Bank to recover the amount of a check that First Credit believes was altered. The check was drawn on Commerce Bank's Christmas Club account with First Credit Bank. Commerce was the depositary bank. A favorable outcome is anticipated in this case.

The remaining proceeding, which involves First National Bank of Dallas, presents a moderate level of risk to the bank because it has subjected the bank to litigation in a state where the bank does not ordinarily conduct business (i.e., Texas). It also presents risks outside the normal course of business, because it has involved the bank in a dispute with FNB of Dallas, which is claiming that First Credit Bank has better advertisements and is "stealing" market share from FNB. A favorable outcome is anticipated in this case.

None of the pending material legal proceedings had amounts at risk in excess of $250,000, excluding attorneys' fees.

The bank incurred approximately $17,000 in legal fees in connection with the one case that was resolved during the quarter and resulted in an unfavorable outcome for the bank. In that case, the 12th Circuit Court determined that management could not enforce a policy banning facial hair for the bank's male employees.

REPUTATION RISK

A review of the bank's most recent regulatory reports failed to identify any repeated adverse regulatory comments made of either the bank or management. Management has a good record of correcting problems identified by the bank's regulators, and any deficiencies in management information systems are considered minor.

Two employees (one at First Credit Bank and the other at the company's Service Corporation) were severely reprimanded for using profanities in front of a customer in the bank's lobby. One employee's remarks were published in the local paper and summarized in the local church bulletin. Nevertheless, the impact to the bank's reputation was minimal, and there was no evidence of any adverse customer (or public) opinion. Both employees have apologized to all bystanders and employees. This issue is no longer a concern.

Management maintains a good rapport with the local media and has not been contacted by consumer groups or political activists questioning the banks strategic plan or business practices.

STRATEGIC RISK

The company's overall strategic risk is considered to be moderate and stable. The rating is based largely on regulatory review findings, until recently the lack of a parent company CEO, and the results of various self-monitoring programs that are reported to the Risk Management Division. A corporate strategic plan is being drafted, and organizational and cultural changes continue.

Strategic risk assessment involves identifying and evaluating all risks that threaten achieving business strategies or enhancing shareholder value. Initially, our strategic risk rating will be largely intuitive and biased in favor of the composite of other risk ratings. However, as the process evolves, a better starting point will likely be to consider quantifiable measures that will affect shareholder value drivers, such as earnings consistency, competitive advantage, efficiency, and capital use, as well as qualifiable measures, such as management, regulatory compliance (including BSA, CRA, and legal), and reputation risks.

NOTES

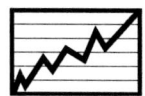

1. Frank Wharton, "Risk Management: Basic Concepts and General Principles," *Risk: Analysis, Assessment, and Management* by Jake Ansell and Frank Wharton (Chichester, UK: John Wiley & Sons, 1992), 4.
2. James W. DeLoach, *Enterprise-wide Risk Management: Strategies for Linking Risk and Opportunity* (London, UK: Pearson Education Limited, 2000), xiii; and Thomas L. Barton, William G. Shenkir, and Paul L. Walker, *Making Enterprise Risk Management Pay Off* (Upper Saddle River, NJ: Financial Times/Prentice Hall PTR, 2002), 5.
3. Remarks by Federal Reserve Governor Susan Schmidt Bies at the Risk Management Association and Consumer Bankers Association Retail Risk Conference, Chicago, IL, July 16, 2004, http://www.federalreserve.gov/BoardDocs/Speeches/2004/20040716/default.htm (accessed August 4, 2005).
4. William J. McDonough, former president and CEO of the Federal Reserve Board of New York and former chairman of the Basel committee, remarks made at the 2003 Legal and Compliance Conference, New York, NY: February 4, 2003.
5. Marc Intrater, "Basel II for Non-Basel II Banks," *Bank Accounting and Finance* (November–December 2004), 7.
6. Ibid, 3.
7. Damian Paletta, "Basel II Survey Finds More Cost, Less Confidence," *American Banker*, July 26, 2005, 4.
8. Kevin S. Buehler, Vijay D'Silva, and Gunnar Pritsch, "The Business Case for Basel II," *The McKinsey Quarterly* (2004 Number 1), 88.

9. Peter L. Bernstein, *Against the Gods: The Remarkable Story of Risk* (New York, NY: John Wiley and Sons, 1998), 18.
10. Matt Siegel, "The Perils of Culture Conflict," *Fortune* (9 November 1998), 258.
11. Art Kleiner, "The Customer Comes Eighth," *Across the Board* (September–October 2003), 17.
12. Glyn A. Holton, "A New Position on Risk," *Futures and Options World* (February 2004), 44.
13. Remarks by Governor Susan Schmidt Bies at the Risk Management Association and Consumer Bankers Association Retail Risk Conference, Chicago, IL, July 16, 2004, http://www.federalreserve.gov/BoardDocs/Speeches/2004/20040716/default.htm (accessed August 4, 2005).
14. "Loan Portfolio Management," Comptroller of the Currency, Comptrollers Handbook Revised April 1998, 37.
15. "Institution Compliance Programs", Federal Deposit Insurance Corporation, FDIC Compliance Handbook Revised July 31, 1999, Appendix B, B-3.
16. "Interagency Policy Statement on the Internal Audit Function and its Outsourcing," Board of Governors of the Federal Reserve System, Comptroller of the Currency, Federal Deposit Insurance Corporation and Office of Thrift Supervision (March 17, 2003), 3.
17. The Institute of Internal Auditors, "The Role of Internal Audit in Enterprise-wide Risk Management," Position Paper, September 29, 2004.
18. Ibid.
19. Institute of Internal Auditors Code of Ethics, http://www.theiia.org/index.cfm?doc_id=604 (accessed August 16, 2005).
20. Interagency Policy Statement on the Internal Audit Function and Its Outsourcing dated March 17, 2003 issued by the Board of Governors of the Federal Reserve System, the Federal

Deposit Insurance Corporation, the Office of the Comptroller of the Currency, and the Office of Thrift Supervision.
21. Interagency Policy Statement on the Internal Audit Function and Its Outsourcing dated March 17, 2003, issued by the Board of Governors of the Federal Reserve System, the Federal Deposit Insurance Corporation, the Office of the Comptroller of the Currency, and the Office of Thrift Supervision.
22. Eric Banfield, "Escalating Risk Visibility: The Professional risk Management View of the Role of the CRO" (Chicago, www.riskcenter.com, November 17, 2005), 2 (accessed November 20, 2005).
23. Ibid., 1.
24. Extracted from Standard & Poor's Annual Global Corporate Default Study, Table 8: Average One-Year Transition Rates 1981 to 2004 (%) and Table 12: Cumulative Average Default Rates by Geographic Region 1981 to 2004 (%).
25. When the author (Karen Van de Castle) first reviewed this matrix (developed by Dr. Bill Chambers, Boston University) with a class of Federal Reserve Bank supervisors, who were regulators overseeing some of the largest financial institutions in the world, the approximately 25 people in the class appreciated the simplicity of this approach. At that time, no one in the class had seen a bank undertake this exercise, but many of the examiners agreed it would be a worthwhile exercise for bank management to undertake.
26. James W. DeLoach, *Enterprise-wide Risk Management: Strategies for Linking Risk and Opportunity* (London, UK: Pearson Education Limited, 2000), 254.
27. Robert S. Dunnett, Cindy B. Levy, and Antonio P. Simoes, "Managing Operational Risk in Banking," *The McKinsey Quarterly* (2005, Number 1), 9.
28. Kevin Dowd, *Measuring Market Risk*, Second Edition (West Sussex, UK: John Wiley & Sons, 2005), 15.

29. James Lam, *Enterprise Risk Management: From Incentives to Controls* (Hoboken, NJ: John Wiley & Sons, 2003), 187–188.
30. Philippe Jorion, *Value at Risk: The New Benchmark for Managing Financial Risk,* Second Edition (New York: McGraw-Hill, 2001), 16.
31. Timothy W. Koch, *Bank Management,* 3rd Edition (Fort Worth, Texas: The Dryden Press, 1995), 108.
32. Michele A. Kreisler and Richard B. Worley, "Value Measures for Managing Interest-Rate Risk," *Perspectives on Interest Rate Risk Management for Money Managers and Traders,* Frank J. Fabozzi, editor (New Hope, Pennsylvania: Frank J. Fabozzi Associates, 1998), 101.
33. James W. Henderson and Terry S. Maness, *The Financial Analyst's Deskbook: A Cash Flow Approach to Liquidity* (New York: Van Nostrand Reinhold, 1989), 95.
34. Jorion, xxiv.
35. Gerd Gigerenzer, *Calculated Risks: How to Know When Numbers Deceive You* (New York, NY: Simon & Schuster, 2002), 42.
36. Ibid.
37. Dowd, 32.
38. Ibid., 33.
39. §644 of *International Convergence of Capital Measurement and Capital Standards* (Basel II).
40. There are some exceptions to this rule, such as settlement failures of marketable securities.
41. In reality, your risk would be closer to zero because the million dollars would be lost with almost 100% certainty.
42. "Legal/Reputational Risks," Federal Reserve Bank of Chicago, http://www.chicagofed.org/banking_information/legal_reputational_risk.cfm (accessed August 20, 2005).
43. "Bank Holding Company Rating System," Board of Governors of the Federal Reserve System,

http://www.philadelphiafed.org/publicaffairs/circulars/attachment5632.pdf (accessed September 26, 2005).

44. Rajendra K. Srivastava, Thomas H. McInish, Robert A. Wood, and Anthony J. Capraro (1997), "The Value of Corporate Reputations: Evidence from Equity Markets," *Corporate Reputation Review*, Vol. 1, No. 1, 62–66.

45. Morten Thannng Vendelo (1998), "Narrating Corporate Reputation," *International Studies of Management and Organization*, Vol. 28, No. 3, 120–137.

46. Manto Gotsi and Alan M. Wilson (2001), "Corporate Reputation: Seeking a Definition," *Corporate Communication: An International Journal*, Vol. 6, No. 1, 24–30.

47. J.B. Baryen (1991), "Firm Resources and Sustained Competitive Advantage," *Journal of Management*, Vol. 17, No. 1, 99–120.

48. Roger Bennett and Rita Kottasz (2000), "Practitioner Perceptions of Corporate Reputation: an Empirical Investigation," *Corporate Communications: An International Journal*, Vol. 5, No. 4, 224–234.

49. Vendelo.

50. John F. Mahon (2002), "Corporate Reputation: A Research Agenda Using Strategy and Stakeholder Literature," *Business and Society*, Vol. 41, No. 4, 415–454.

51. Nha Nguyen and Gaston LeBlanc (2001), "Corporate Image and Corporate Reputation in Customers' Retention Decisions in Services," *Journal of Retailing and Consumer Services*, Vol. 8, No. 1, 227–236.

52. Marvine E. Goldberg and Jon Hartwick (1990), "The Effects of Advertiser Reputation and Extremity of Advertising Claim on Advertising Effectiveness," *Journal of Consumer Research*, Vol. 17, No. 1, 172–179.

53. Charles J. Fombrun and Cees B.M. Van Riel, *Fame & Fortune, How Successful Companies Build Winning Reputations* (Upper Saddle River, NJ: FT Prentice Hall), 10–11, 2004.

54. "Biennial Risk Management and Risk Financing Survey," *Aon*, 2005.

55. *"The Evolution of Risk Management in the Financial Services Industry,"* Pricewaterhouse Coopers and the Economic Intelligence Unit, 2004.

56. Ibid.

57. Gary E. Peterson, *Managing Reputation Risk—Creating an Effective Risk Structure,* Part II, http://www.boardmember.com/network/CorpBdPart2.pdf (accessed July 2, 2005).

58. Jenny Rayner, *Managing Reputational Risk* (West Sussex, UK: John Wiley & Sons, 2003), 47–211.

59. Basel Committee on Banking Supervision, "Compliance and the Compliance Function in Banks," April 29, 2005, http://www.bis.org/publ/bcbs113.pdf, page 3, (accessed September 4, 2005).

60. "A Banker's Guide to Establishing and Maintaining an Effective Compliance Management Program," 2002, the Federal Reserve Bank of Kansas City, http://64.233.161.104/search?q=cache:d-f1HEmq18cJ:www.kc.frb.org/consumer/bankguide.htm (accessed September 25, 2005).

61. Ibid.

62. Paul S. J. Coquillette and S. Andrew Thompson, Jr., "A Banker's Guide to Establishing and Maintaining an Effective Compliance Program," White Paper, 2002, page 3.

63. Remarks by Governor Susan Schmidt Bies at the Bond Market Association's "Legal and Compliance Conference," New York, NY, February 4, 2004, http://www.federalreserve.gov/boarddocs/speeches/2004/20040204/default.htm (accessed September 4, 2005).

64. "Institution Compliance Programs," *FDIC Compliance Handbook,* Appendix B, page B-3, July 31, 1999.

65. Securities and Exchange Commission, 17 CFR Parts 270 and 275, Final Rule: Compliance Programs of Investment Companies and Investment Advisers [Release Nos. IA-2204;

IC-26299; File No. S7-03-03] RIN 3235-AI77, section II C, page 10.
66. Remarks by Governor Susan Schmidt Bies at the Risk Management Association and Consumer Bankers Association Retail Risk Conference, Chicago, IL, July 16, 2004, http://www.federalreserve.gov/BoardDocs/Speeches/2004/20040716/default.htm (accessed August 4, 2005).
67. Adrian J. Slywotzky and John Drzik, "Countering the Biggest Risk of All," *Harvard Business Review* (April 2005), 80.
68. Ali Samad-Khan, "Why COSO is Flawed," *Operational Risk* (January 2005), 1. http://www.opriskadvisory.com/docs/Why%20COSO%20Is%20Inappropriate%20for%20Operational%20Risk%20Management%20(Jan%202005).pdf (accessed August 11, 2005).
69. Julie L. Williams (acting Comptroller of the Currency), "Acting Comptroller Williams Discusses Management and Supervision of Reputation Risk in Large Banking Organizations; Stresses Important Role of Ethics and Corporate Values," *OCC Press Releases,* http://www.occ.treas.gov/toolkit/newsrelease.aspx?Doc=AJX421LZ.xml (accessed May 6, 2005).
70. J. David Cummins (The Wharton School), Lewis, Christopher M. (The Hartford Insurance Group), Wei, Ran (The Wharton School), "The Market Value Impact of Operational Risk Events for U.S. Banks and Insurers," December 23, 2004.
71. "Decision Makers: Inside the Operating Room," *NPR's Morning Edition,* April 12, 2005, http://www.npr.org/templates/story/story.php?storyId=4586808 (assessed August 3, 2005).
72. Tammy DeMel, "Measuring Enterprise Risk Management," *State of Business* (Spring 2005), 14.
73. Philippe Jorion, *Value at Risk: The New Benchmark for Managing Financial Risk,* Second Edition (New York, NY: McGraw Hill, 2001), 485.

74. Kevin Dowd, *Measuring Market Risk* (West Sussex, UK: John Wiley & Sons, 2002), 8.
75. Over the past three decades, there have been a number of text written on VAR. This is not one of them. For the comprehensive explanation and discussion of VAR, seek guidance from the statistical experts such as Philippe Jorion in *Value at Risk: The New Benchmark for Managing Financial Risk*, Second Edition (New York, NY: McGraw Hill, 2001) and Kevin Dowd, *Measuring Market Risk*, Second Edition (West Sussex, UK: John Wiley & Sons, 2005).
76. Jorion, 10.
77. Kevin Dowd, *Measuring Market Risk*, Second Edition (West Sussex, UK: John Wiley & Sons, 2005), 5.
78. Scott F. Richard, and Benjamin J. Gord, "Measuring and Managing Interest Rate Risk," *Perspectives on Interest Rate Risk Management for Money Managers and Trader*, Frank J. Fabozzi, Editor (New Hope, PA: Frank J. Fabozzi Associates, 1998), 89.
79. Dowd.
80. Norman Jackson and Pippa Carter, "The Perception of Risk," *Risk: Analysis, Assessment, and Management* by Jake Ansell and Frank Wharton (Chichester, UK: John Wiley & Sons, 1992), 47.
81. Linda Allen, Jacob Boudoukh, and Anthony Saunders, *Understanding Market, Credit, and Operational Risk: The Value at Risk Approach* (Malden, MA: Blackwell Publishing, 2004), 159.
82. Jorion, 29.
83. *The Ernst & Young Guide to Performance Measurement for Financial Institutions: Methods for Managing Business Results*, Revised Edition (New York, NY: McGraw-Hill, 1995), 219.

84. Don Powell, "Remarks by FDIC Chairman Don Powell at the FDIC's Center for Financial Research—Spring Risk Management & Derivatives Conference, April 8, 2005. http://www.fdic.gov/news/news/ press/2005/pr3305.html (accessed September 25, 2005).
85. Ibid.
86. ERisk, "Economic Capital and RAROC Primer," White Paper, http://erisk.com/Learning/ EconCap/econcap1.asp (accessed September 25, 2005).
87. Robert L. Burns, "Economic Capital and the Assessment of Capital Adequacy," *The RMA Journal,* April 2005, 55.
88. *The Ernst & Young Guide to Performance Measurement for Financial Institutions,* 223.
89. Burns, 62.
90. Todd Warren and Adel Mamhikoff, "Risk-Adjusted Measurement," *CFO Project,* Volume 2, October 1, 2003, 283.

GLOSSARY

Basel II. A framework that outlines procedures for regulating capital allocations against credit, operational, and market risk endorsed by worldwide central bank governors and the heads of bank supervisory authorities in the Group of Ten (G10) countries (see the Basel framework at bis.org).

Chief compliance officer (CCO). Generally responsible for assessing and managing compliance or regulatory risks.

Chief risk officer (CRO). Generally responsible for a company's risk management activities and results. Role includes being spokesperson about the company's risks.

COSO. The Committee of Sponsoring Organizations of the Treadway Commission. COSO is a voluntary private sector organization dedicated to improving financial reporting through business ethics, effective internal controls, and corporate governance (see COSO.org).

Credit risk. Generally defined as the risk due to uncertainty in a counter-party's ability to perform on a credit obligation. Credit risk results from any uncertainty in a counter-party's ability to meet its obligations.

EAD. *See* exposure at default.

Economic capital. The amount of equity capital necessary to cover potential losses, at a specific risk level, over a specific period of time.

Economic profit. The profit earned after deducting operating expenses and a charge for the opportunity cost of the capital employed. *See also* shareholder value-added (SVA).

Economic value-added. An absolute performance measure that, like RAROC, takes into account expected as well as unexpected losses. It is calculated using the formula: (EVA = Income − Claims − Costs) or (EVA = ΔEL − Cost of capital).

Enterprise risk management (ERM). A business strategy that combines mitigating and managing the negative consequences that occur within normal business operations with the proper balance of profitability and risk. It is also the holistic management of all genres of risk across the company.

Exchange risk. The chance that a nation's currency will lose value when exchanged for foreign currencies.

Expected loss. The average loss associated with some activity—most typically it represents expected loss from defaulting loans or from operational risk.

Exposure at default (EAD). The amount currently drawn on a credit and an estimate of future draw downs of available but untapped credit. EAD generally applies to nonterm exposures only, such as unfunded loan commitments and lines of credit.

Federal Deposit Insurance Corporation (FDIC). The agency of the federal government established to provide insurance protection, up to statutory limits, for depositors at FDIC member institutions. All national banks and all Fed member banks must belong to the FDIC; other commercial banks and savings banks may join also.

Hurdle rate. A required rate of return. In risk management, the hurdle rate is measured in terms of risk-adjusted return.

Inflation risk. The danger that the dollars one invests today will buy less in the future because prices of consumer goods rise. A continuing increase in the level of

Glossary

prices in an economy, caused by too many dollars and too few goods to be purchased.

Interest rate risk. The risk that the value of an asset or liability will change resulting from a change in interest rates.

LGD. *See* loss given default.

Legal risk. A risk that arises from the potential that changes in the law, unenforceable contracts, legal proceedings, or illegal or unethical conduct can disrupt or otherwise negatively affect the operations or condition of the bank.

Liquidity risk. The risk that an investment, when converted to cash, will experience loss in its value.

Loss given default (LGD). The credit loss incurred if a borrower fails to fully repay the loan. It is based on collateral value, seniority, and the bank's loss-recovery history. LGD also may be expressed as (1 − Recovery rate).

Market risk. The possibility of loss due to adverse movement in the interest rates, foreign exchange rates, commodity prices, or equity prices.

New Basel Capital Accord. *See* Basel II.

Operational risk. The risk of loss resulting from inadequate or failed internal processes, people and systems, or from external events.

OCC. Office of the Comptroller of the Currency, administrator of national banks.

OTS. Office of Thrift Supervision, administrator of savings banks and thrifts.

PD. *See* probability of default.

Probability of default (PD). The likelihood that a loan will not be repaid and fall into default. In Basel II, several events may constitute a default. However, once a borrower becomes 90 days delinquent, the credit is firmly in default.

RAROC. *See* risk adjusted return on capital.

Reinvestment risk. The danger that reinvested money will fetch returns lower than those earned before reinvestment. Individuals with dividend-reinvestment plans are subject to this risk. Bondholders are subjects to this risk as well.

Regulatory capital. The amount of capital required by a bank's regulators.

Regulatory risk. The risk associated with the failure to comply with laws related to banking and related practices.

Reputation risk. The reduced market value or constituent perception as a result of an organization's or its competitors' past, current, or future business practices.

Risk-adjusted return on capital (RAROC). A profitability calculation used to measure risk-adjusted financial performance in relation to capital.

Risk management. The process of assessing risk, taking steps to reduce risk to an acceptable level, maintaining that level of risk, and reporting risks to the bank's senior management and the board.

Shareholder value-added (SVA). The profit earned after deducting operating expenses, and a charge for the opportunity cost of the capital employed. *See also* economic profit.

Strategic risk. The risk to earnings or capital arising from adverse business decisions or improper implementation of decisions.

Unexpected loss. The potential for actual loss to exceed the expected loss; a measure of the uncertainty inherent in the loss estimate.

Value-at-risk (VAR). The maximum percentage of value likely to be gained or lost as the result of normal price movement over a given period of time.

BIBLIOGRAPHY

Allen, Linda, and Anthony Saunders. *Credit Risk Measurement: New Approaches to Value at Risk and Other Paradigms*, Second Edition. New York, NY: John Wiley & Sons, 2002.

Allen, Linda, Jacob Boudoukh, and Anthony Saunders. *Understanding Market, Credit, and Operational Risk: The Value at Risk Approach*. Malden, MA: Blackwell Publishing Ltd, 2004.

Ansell, Jake, and Frank Wharton. *Risk: Analysis, Assessment, and Management*. Chichester, UK: John Wiley & Sons, 1992.

Banfield, Eric. "Escalating Risk Visibility: The Professional Risk Management View of the Role of the CRO." RiskCenter.com. Chicago, IL: November 17, 2005 (accessed November 20, 2005).

"Bank Holding Company Rating System." Board of Governors of the Federal Reserve System. http://www.philadelphiafed.org/publicaffairs/circulars/attachment5632.pdf (accessed September 26, 2005).

"Banker's Guide to Establishing and Maintaining an Effective Compliance Management Program." Federal Reserve Bank of Kansas City, 2002. http://64.233.161.104/search?q=cache:d-f1HEmq18cJ:www.kc.frb.org/consumer/bankguide.htm (accessed September 25, 2005).

Barton, Thomas L., William G. Shenkir, and Paul L. Walker. *Making Enterprise Risk Management Pay Off: How Leading Companies Implement Risk Management*. Upper Saddle River, NJ: Financial Times/Prentice Hall PTR, 2002.

Baryen, J.B. "Firm Resources and Sustained Competitive Advantage." *Journal of Management*, Vol. 17, No. 1 (1991): 99–120.

Bennett, Roger, and Rita Kottasz. "Practitioner Perceptions of Corporate Reputation: An Empirical Investigation." *Corporate Communications: An International Journal,* Vol. 5, No. 4 (2000): 224–234.

Bernstein, Peter L. *Against the Gods: The Remarkable Story of Risk.* New York, NY: John Wiley and Sons, 1998.

"Biennial Risk Management and Risk Financing Survey," *Aon,* 2005.

Bies, Susan Schmidt, "Remarks by Governor Susan Schmidt Bies at the Risk Management Association and Consumer Bankers Association Retail Risk Conference," Chicago, IL: July 16, 2004. http://www.federalreserve.gov/BoardDocs/Speeches/2004/20040716/default.htm (accessed August 4, 2005).

Bies, Susan Schmidt. Remarks by Governor Susan Schmidt Bies at the Bond Market Association's "Legal and Compliance Conference." New York, NY: February 4, 2004. http://www.federalreserve.gov/boarddocs/speeches/2004/20040204/default.htm (accessed September 4, 2005).

"The Big Mac Index." *Economist.com.* http://www.economist.com/markets/Bigmac/Index.cfm (accessed August 24, 2005).

Bird, Anat, and Tara Heusé Skinner. "Enterprise Risk Management Not for You? Wrong." *American Banker* (April 8, 2005): 10.

Blue Ribbon Committee on Improving the Effectiveness of Corporate Audit Committees. Report and Recommendations of the Blue Ribbon Committee on Improving the Effectiveness of Corporate Audit Committee Reports, 1999, reprinted in 54 BUS. LAW. 1067, 1073 (1999).

Buehler, Kevin S., Vijay D'Silva, and Gunnar Pritsch. "The Business Case for Basel II." *The McKinsey Quarterly* (2005 Number 1): 83–91.

Burns, Robert L. "Economic Capital and the Assessment of Capital Adequacy." *The RMA Journal* (April 2005): 54–62.

Christensen, Clayton M. *The Innovator's Dilemma*. New York, NY: HarperBusiness, 2000.

Cole, Leonard P. *Management Accounting in Banks*. Rolling Meadows, IL: Bank Administrative Institute, 1988.

"Compliance and the Compliance Function in Banks." Basel Committee on Banking Supervision, April 29, 2005. http://www.bis.org/publ/bcbs113.pdf (accessed September 4, 2005).

Coquillette, Paul S. J., and S. Andrew Thompson, Jr. "A Banker's Guide to Establishing and Maintaining an Effective Compliance Program," White Paper, 2002. http://64.233.161.104/search?q=cache:d-f1HEmq18cJ:www.kc.frb.org/consumer/bankguide.htm (accessed September 25, 2005).

Crouhy, Michel, Dan Galai, and Robert Mark. *Risk Management*. New York, NY: McGraw-Hill, 2001.

Cummins, J. David (The Wharton School), Lewis, Christopher M. (The Hartford Insurance Group), Wei, Ran (The Wharton School), "The Market Value Impact of Operational Risk Events for U.S. Banks and Insurers," December 23, 2004.

de Servigny, Arnaud, and Olivier Renault. *Measuring and Managing Credit Risk*. New York, NY: McGraw-Hill, 2004.

"Decision Makers: Inside the Operating Room," NPR's Morning Edition, April 12, 2005. http://www.npr.org/templates/story/story.php?storyId=4586808 (accessed August 3, 2005).

DeLoach, James W. *Enterprise-wide Risk Management: Strategies for Linking Risk and Opportunity*. London, UK: Pearson Education Limited, 2000.

DeMel, Tammy. "Measuring Enterprise Risk Management." *State of Business* (Spring 2005): 12–14.

Dowd, Kevin. *Measuring Market Risk*, Second Edition. West Sussex, UK: John Wiley & Sons, 2005.

Dowd, Kevin. *Measuring Market Risk*. West Sussex, UK: John Wiley & Sons, 2002.

Dunnett, Robert S., Cindy B. Levy, and Antonio P. Simoes. "Managing Operational Risk in Banking," *The McKinsey Quarterly* (2005, Number 1): 9–11.

"Economic Capital & RAROC Primer," *Erisk,* July 13, 2005. http://erisk.com/Learning/EconCap/econcap1.asp (accessed September 25, 2005).

"The Evolution of Risk Management in the Financial Services Industry," Pricewaterhouse Coopers and the Economic Intelligence Unit, 2004.

Flaherty, Thomas J., Todd J. Jirovec, and Dwight L. Allen. "No Surprises," *Electric Perspectives* (November–December 2002). http://www.findarticles.com/ p/articles/mi_qa3650/is_200211/ai_n9091333 (accessed August 3, 2005).

Fombrun, Charles J., and Cees B.M. Van Riel. *Fame & Fortune, How Successful Companies Build Winning Reputations.* Upper Saddle River, NJ: FT Prentice Hall, 2004.

Gigerenzer, Gerd. *Calculated Risks: How to Know When Numbers Deceive You.* New York, NY: Simon & Schuster, 2002.

Githens, Bill. "Fifth Third's Preparation for Takeoff." *The RMA Journal* (March 2005): 8–15.

Goldberg, Marvine E., and Jon Hartwick. "The Effects of Advertiser Reputation and Extremity of Advertising Claim on Advertising Effectiveness." *Journal of Consumer Research,* Vol. 17, No. 1 (1990): 172–179.

Gotsi, Manto, and Alan M. Wilson. "Corporate Reputation: Seeking a Definition." *Corporate Communication: An International Journal,* Vol. 6, No. 1 (2001): 24–30.

Henderson, James W., and Terry S. Maness. *The Financial Analyst's Deskbook: A Cash Flow Approach to Liquidity.* New York, NY: Van Nostrand Reinhold, 1989.

Holton, Glyn A. "A New Position on Risk." *Futures and Options World* (February 2004): 44–45.

"Institution Compliance Programs." *FDIC Compliance Handbook.* Appendix B, page B-3, July 31, 1999

Institute of Internal Auditors Code of Ethics. http://www.theiia.org/index.cfm?doc_id=604 (accessed August 16, 2005).

"Interagency Policy Statement on the Internal Audit Function and its Outsourcing." Board of Governors of the Federal Reserve System, Comptroller of the Currency, Federal Deposit Insurance Corporation, and Office of Thrift Supervision. (March 17, 2003).

Intrater, Marc. "Basel II for Non-Basel II Banks." *Bank Accounting and Finance* (October–November 2004): 3–9.

Jackson, Norman, and Pippa Carter, "The Perception of Risk," *Risk: Analysis, Assessment, and Management* by Jake Ansell and Frank Wharton. Chichester, UK: John Wiley & Sons, 1992.

Jorion, Philippe. *Value at Risk: The New Benchmark for Managing Financial Risk,* Second Edition. New York, NY: McGraw Hill, 2001.

Kleiner, Art. "The Customer Comes Eighth." *Across the Board* (September–October 2003): 16–22.

Koch, Timothy W. *Bank Management,* 3rd Edition. Fort Worth, Texas: The Dryden Press, 1995.

Kreisler, Michele A., and Richard B. Worley. "Value Measures for Managing Interest-Rate Risk." *Perspectives on Interest Rate Risk Management for Money Managers and Traders.* Fabozzi, Frank J., editor. New Hope, PA: Frank J. Fabozzi Associates, 1998, pages 101–112.

Lam, James. *Enterprise Risk Management: From Incentives to Controls.* Hoboken, NJ: John Wiley & Sons, 2003.

"Loan Portfolio Management." *Comptrollers Handbook.* (April 1998).

"Legal/Reputational Risks." Federal Reserve Bank of Chicago. http://www.chicagofed.org/banking_information/legal_reputational_risk.cfm (accessed August 20, 2005).

Mahon, John F. "Corporate Reputation: A Research Agenda Using Strategy and Stakeholder Literature." *Business and Society,* Vol. 41, No. 4 (2002): 415–454.

McDonough, William J. Remarks made at the 2003 Legal and Compliance Conference, New York, NY (February 4, 2003).

Nguyen, Nha, and Gaston LeBlanc. "Corporate Image and Corporate Reputation in Customers' Retention Decisions in Services." *Journal of Retailing and Consumer Services*, Vol. 8, No. 1 (2001): 227–236.

Olson, Kim, and Martin Hansen, *Demystifying Basel II: A Closer Look at the IRB Measures and Disclosure Framework*, Fitch Ratings, August 25, 2004.

Paletta, Damian. "Basel II Survey Finds More Cost, Less Confidence." *American Banker.* (July 26, 2005): 4.

Peterson, Gary E. "Managing Reputation Risk—Creating an Effective Risk Structure," Part II. http://www.boardmember.com/network/CorpBdPart2.pdf (accessed July 2, 2005).

Powell, Don. "Remarks by FDIC Chairman Don Powell at the FDIC's Center For Financial Research—Spring Risk Management & Derivatives Conference, April 8, 2005. http://www.fdic.gov/news/news/press/2005/pr3305.html (accessed September 25, 2005).

Ramos, Michael. *How to Comply with Sarbanes-Oxley Section 404: Assessing the Effectiveness of Internal Control.* Hoboken, NJ: John Wiley & Sons, 2004.

Rayner, Jenny. *Managing Reputational Risk.* West Sussex, UK, 2003.

Richard, Scott F., and Benjamin J. Gord. "Measuring and Managing Interest Rate Risk." *Perspectives on Interest Rate Risk Management for Money Managers and Traders.* Frank J. Fabozzi, Editor. New Hope, PA: Frank J. Fabozzi Associates, 1998, pages 89–99.

Samad-Khan, Ali. "Why COSO is Flawed." *Operational Risk* (January 2005). http://www.opriskadvisory.com/docs/ [Why COSO Is Inappropriate for Operational Risk Management (Jan 2005)] pdf (accessed August 11, 2005).

Schelling, Thomas. "The Role of War Games and Exercises," *Managing Nuclear Options.* Ashton B. Carter and John D. Steinbruner, authors, and Charles A. Zraket, editor. Washington DC: Brookings Institution, 1987: 436.

Securities and Exchange Commission, 17 CFR Parts 270 and 275, Final Rule: Compliance Programs of Investment Companies and Investment Advisers, [Release Nos. IA-2204; IC-26299; File No. S7-03-03] RIN 3235-AI77.

Siegel, Matt. "The Perils of Culture Conflict." *Fortune* (9 November 1998): 257–262.

Slywotzky, Adrian J., and John Drzik. "Countering the Biggest Risk of All," *Harvard Business Review* (April 2005): 78–88.

Srivastava, Rajendra K., Thomas H. McInish, Robert A. Wood, and Anthony J. Capraro. "The Value of Corporate Reputations: Evidence from Equity Markets," *Corporate Reputation Review,* Vol. 1, No. 1 (1997): 62–66.

The Ernst & Young Guide to Performance Measurement for Financial Institutions: Methods for Managing Business Results, Revised Edition. New York, NY: McGraw-Hill, 1995.

The Institute of Internal Auditors, "The Role of Internal Audit in Enterprise-wide Risk Management," Position Paper, September 29, 2004.

Vazza, Dianne, Devi Aurora, and Ryan Schneck, Standard & Poor's *Annual Global Corporate Default Study: Corporate Defaults Poised to Rise in 2005,* January 2005.

Vendelo, Morten Thanning. "Narrating Corporate Reputation." *International Studies of Management and Organization,* Vol. 28, No. 3 (1998): 120–137.

Warren, Todd, and Adel Mamhikoff. "Risk-Adjusted Measurement." *CFO Project.* Vol. 2, October 1, 2003: 283–286.

Wharton, Frank. "Risk Management: Basic Concepts and General Principles." *Risk: Analysis, Assessment, and Management* by Jake Ansell and Frank Wharton. Chichester, UK: John Wiley & Sons, 1992.

Williams, Julie L. (Acting Comptroller of the Currency). "Acting Comptroller Williams Discusses Management and Supervision of Reputation Risk in Large Banking Organizations; Stress Important role of Ethics and Corporate Values." OCC Press Releases, http://www.occ.treas.gov/toolkit/newsrelease.aspx? Doc=AJX421LZ.xml (accessed May 6, 2005).

ABOUT THE CONTRIBUTORS

Contributing Editors

Robert Oberg is Senior Vice President and Chief Risk Officer for First Financial Bancorp. He is responsible for risk identification, assessment, and management throughout the organization. Specifically, he is responsible for risk quantification and modeling, developing and implementing policies and risk-adjusted performance measurements, assessing the relative efficiency of business units in creating value, developing economic capital techniques to support capital allocation, and developing enterprise-wide risk strategies. Concurrent with his risk management position at First Financial Bancorp, Robert is a member of national risk management roundtables, serves on the board of directors of the Risk Management Association's Cincinnati Chapter, is on the faculty of ABA's Stonier Graduate School of banking at Georgetown University, and is an occasional lecturer on credit policy, administration, and risk management for universities, industry conferences, and trade associations. A graduate of Oklahoma State University, he holds degrees in economics, political science, and pre-law.

Tara Heusé Skinner is Executive Vice President and the Chief Risk Officer of The South Financial Group, Inc. where she serves on several high-level risk management committees. She is a member of numerous ERM networking and peer groups and is published on the enterprise risk management topic. She speaks on the fundamentals of ERM and its implementation challenges in various conferences and Webcasts. She chairs the Conference Board's Strategic Risk Management Council's Executive Committee. Tara, who holds an MBA from Louisiana State University, is a distinguished graduate of ABA's Stonier Graduate School of Banking. She now serves on its board of advisors and its faculty. Tara is currently pursuing a doctorate with the International School of Management in Paris.

Contributors

Anat Bird is Chairman and Chief Executive Officer of SCB Forums, LTD., a company that arranges and facilitates peer group meetings for bank CEOs. She has held senior executive positions at Wells Fargo, Norwest, and Roosevelt Financial. Anat is a Professor at U.C. Davis, where she teaches an MBA course on Financial Markets and Institutions, and a faculty member for the CSUS Executive Education program. She received a Diploma in Corporate Strategic Planning from the Wharton School of Business, an MBA in Finance with High Honors from American University in Washington, DC, and an M.A. in International Relations from Hebrew University in Jerusalem. She is the author of over 400 articles, has given over 300 speeches, and has written seven books. Currently, she serves on the board of directors for four banks.

Ali Samad-Khan is President of OpRisk Advisory LLC, a leading operational risk management consulting firm. He has extensive experience in operational risk management and is widely regarded as an industry thought-leader. He has assisted more than a dozen of the world's leading financial institutions in establishing operational risk management programs. Frequently, he is invited to advise and train the major bank regulatory authorities, including the Basel Committee on Banking Supervision, on operational risk measurement, and management issues. Dozens of leading financial institutions worldwide have adopted key elements of his operational risk management framework/methodology. These key elements also have been incorporated into the Basel II standards. Ali holds a B.A. in Quantitative Economics from Stanford University and an MBA. in Finance from Yale University.

Ladd Muzzy is a director of risk management at Aon, a diversified management consulting and insurance corporation. Over the past 10 years, he has worked in and consulted for some of the world's largest financial institutions. His primary responsibility is to develop and implement enterprise risk management frameworks. These include developing and implementing reputation risk methodologies, development of economic capital models for operational risk, Basel II coordination, and strategic risk analytics. He holds an MBA in strategy, marketing, and finance from Northwestern University's Kellogg Graduate School of Business and a mathematics degree from the University of Michigan.

Granger Souder, Executive Vice President, General Counsel, and Corporate Secretary of Sky Financial Group, Inc., serves as chair of the officer's risk management group, Sky's enterprise risk-oversight body. Granger holds a B.A. from Wittenberg University and a J.D. from the University of Toledo College of Law. He also graduated from the Graduate School of Banking at the University of Wisconsin at Madison.

Maria Tabrizi, Group Senior Vice President and Director of Audit and Advisory Services for Cole Taylor Bank since 1992, directs its internal audit function. She manages its Sarbanes Oxley Section 404 compliance process and is a member of its risk management and disclosure review committees. Prior to joining Cole Taylor Bank, Maria was director of financial reporting for computer software developer Infortext Systems, Inc. Previously, Maria was an audit supervisor for the certified public accounting firm of Laventhol and Horwath. Maria is a certified public accountant and certified risk professional. She holds a BBA degree with a major in public accounting from Loyola University of Chicago. Maria is a member of the American Institute of Certified Public Accountants (CPA), Illinois CPA Society, and the Institute of Internal Auditors (IIA). She also is a member of the IIA Northwest Metro Chicago Chapter's Board of Governors.

Karen Van de Castle is Senior Vice President at GE Capital Market Services, where she leads market analytics. She has more than 20 years of academic and practical experience in credit risk management. Prior to joining GE, she was a consultant for Standard & Poor's Risk Solutions and focused on helping banks refine their internal rating systems. In this role, she was responsible for benchmarking risk practices of commercial banks worldwide. She is published on the topics of credit risk management, recovery experience in the leveraged finance market, and on evaluating credit risk models. Previously, Karen worked for several banks. She studied finance in the doctoral program at Rutgers University, has an MBA from the University of North Carolina, Chapel Hill, and holds a BBA from the College of William and Mary.

Ruth Yang, Director for Standard & Poor's Leveraged Commentary & Data (LCD) based in New York, is responsible for LCD's analytics for the European market. Her areas of expertise include the S&P European Leveraged Loan Index, as well as the group's portfolio management application, a platform for managing and analyzing individual credits. Ruth originally joined the group in 2000 when it was still Portfolio Management & Data, LLC (PMD). At that time, she focused on loan recovery analysis and research, as well as on the S&P/LSTA Leveraged Loan Index. In 2002, she moved to the Loan Syndications & Trading Association (LSTA) as director of market data, overseeing mark-to-market processes. She returned to LCD in 2004. Ruth was educated at Harvard University, and attended graduate studies at the University of Colorado, Boulder.

INDEX

A

Accounting-based loss provision, 130
Acquisitions, risk profile, 9
Activities, risk profile, 9
Advanced-risk methodology, U.S. federal banking agency determination, 7
Advertising, beliefs (improvement), 93
Advocacy groups, action, 115
Aggregate loss distributions, usage, 88
AIG, aberrations, 117
Allied Irish, scandal, 17
AML issues, 17
AmSouth Bank, 43
  regulation violations, 17
Analytics
  addition. *See* Risk
  providing, 22
Anti-default bets, 57
Anti-Money Laundering Regulations, 99
Arthur Andersen, aberrations, 117
Asset modeling, supplantation, 36
Asset portfolio amount, liability portfolio amount (difference), 129
Asset quality. *See* Business
  description, 65
  improvement, 8
Audit
  axioms, 40–44
  ERM, emergence (problem), 47

B

Banfield, Eric, 48
Bank culture
  characteristics, determination, 16
  ERM relationship, 13
  implementation strategy, matching, 13
  relationship. *See* Enterprise risk management
  risk awareness, 15
  success, formula, 13
  typing, 16
Bank for International Settlements, Basel Capital Accord, 6–7
Bank Holding Company Rating System. *See* Federal Reserve
Bank risk
  assessment, 25
  functions, 20–21
  identification, 37
  measurement, 11
  profile, 10
  understanding, 49, 53–54, 69
Bank Secrecy Act (BSA), 98, 99
  independent review, 101
  issues, 17
  officer, 105
  program, 39
Banking
  organization, economic incentives, 3
  regulators, requirements, 29
  risk, measurement, 132

215

Banks
  business, threats (focus), 17–18
  compliance
    function, 39
    program, long-term strategic-level view (development), 102
  economic benefits, 5
  ERM function, CEO endorsement, 23–24
  examiner, hiring (advantage), 46
  executive. See Enterprise risk management bank executive
    guidance, 59
    obstacles, 15
  external exam findings, 18
  historical lending record, visualization, 63
  internal exam findings, 18
  internal rating
    scale, 63
    system, 65
  IT, operational risk, 83
  market value, risk events (impact), 117
  net interest income, variability, 72
  personnel, success (characteristics), 16
  portfolio
    asset level, 128
    credit migration, 65–66
  probabilities, calculation, 15
  rating, increase, 10
  regulators, 45
    relationship, 104
    risk management opportunity, 46
  risk appetite, 42
  risk integration
    measurement, usage, 125
    success, formula, 126
  strategic planning, 36
    process, 32
Barings, scandal, 17
Basel Accord, adoption, 6
Basel Capital Accord. See Bank for International Settlements
  drafting. See New Basel Capital Accord
Basel II
  adoption, 7
  application, 7–8
  banks, problems. See Non-Basel II banks
  compliance, 131
  definition. See Exposure at default
  expansion, 6
  focus. See Operational risk
  measures, 135
  provisions, 5, 6
Basel lite, 8
Benchmarks. See Risk
  establishment, 42
  report, 37
Bies, Susan Schmidt, 38, 107
Big Mac Index, usage, 69
Board of directors
  committee, delegation, 48–50
  definitions. See Risk management
  oversight, 91
  perception. See Risk management
  reports, preparation, 36
  response, 24
  role, 48–50

Index

Borrowers
  creditworthiness, 60
  risk grade, 65
Borrowing entity/obligor, 60
BSA. *See* Bank Secrecy Act
Business
  asset quality, 66
  complexity, recognition, 112
  decisions, 18
  diversification, 22
  lines, revenue streams, 22
  model/objectives, reputation
    risk (impact), 113

C

Capabilities (improvement),
  measurement (impact), 15
Capital adequacy, measure, 140
Capital charges, 61
Capital deficiencies, 17
Capital limit, report, 37
Capital requirements
  decrease, 8
  implications, 21
Capital tiers, 137
Carson, Ben, 118
Catastrophic risk events,
  prediction, 34
Charge-offs, 139
Chief executive officer (CEO)
  appointment, 16
  commitment. *See* Corporate-
    wide initiative
  endorsement. *See* Banks
  knowledge, value, 21
  management style, 23–24
  skepticism. *See* Risk
    management
  vantage point, 23
Chief financial officer (CFO),
  vantage point, 23

Chief risk officer (CRO)
  appointment, value, 37
  hiring/assigning. *See* Full-time
    CRO
  independence, need, 38–40
  locating, 45–47
    avoidance, 47
  qualifications/qualities, 44, 45
  responsibilities, 37–38
    division, avoidance, 46
  role, 36–40
  scorecard, confusion
    (minimization), 48
  senior executive status, 31
  success, 38, 52
Chinese Wall, separation, 42–43
ChoicePoint, complaints
  (filing), 94
City National Bank, 43
Clients/collaborators, 20–22
Collateral, quality, 60
Commerce Bancorp, 43
Commercial banking
  organization, legal risk
    (manifestation), 90
Committee of Sponsoring Organizations of the Tread-
  way Commission (COSO)
  failure, 41
  framework, 127–128
Community Reinvestment Act
  (CRA), 98
  data integrity tests, 101
Competitive advantages
  discovery, 19
  sustenance, 93
Compliance. *See* Corporate
  compliance; Sarbanes-
  Oxley compliance
  culture, 92
  division, 31

Compliance—(*Cont.*)
    function. *See* Banks
    needs, 35
    officer
        activities, 103
        report, 105
    risk, 97
    role, elevation, 18
Confidence deterioration, 97
Confidence level, 77
    explanation, 78
    mathematical explanations, 139
Constituent groups, impact, 115
Consumer compliance
        regulations, 98
Consumer safety, protection
        (value), 96
Controls, addition, 18
Corporate compliance
    function, defining, 98–100
    officer, role, 102–104
Corporate failures, 40
Corporate insurance companies,
        risk management
        perspective, 10
Corporate level, risk
        management, 21
Corporate reputation,
        sustenance, 93
Corporate-wide initiative, CEO
        commitment/executive
        management buy-in,
        19–24
COSO. *See* Committee of Sponsoring Organizations of the Treadway Commission
Cost-benefit analysis, 86
CRA. *See* Community Reinvestment Act
Credit administration, 64–65
Credit risk, 55, 68
    components, 57–61, 68
    division, 31
    exposure, 33
    function, independence, 39
    management, 34–35
        methodologies, 8
    measurement, 131
        methodology, 126
    success, formula, 55–56
CreditProm, 67
Crisis management, 96–97
    plan, updating, 97
    structure, 96
CRO. *See* Chief risk officer
Culture. *See* Bank culture
    change, avoidance, 13
    differentiator, 15
    strategies. *See* Risk-averse
        culture strategies;
        Risk-neutral culture
        strategies; Risk-tolerant
        culture strategies
Currency exchange rates, risk, 69
Customer loyalty, increase, 93

D

De novos, risk profile, 9
Debt cushion, 60
Decision making, 133
    success, formula, 133–134
    tool. *See* Economic capital
Default. *See* Loss given default
    exposure, 60. *See also*
        Exposure at default
    frequency, empirical
        average, 58
    percentage, 61
    probability, 57–59. *See also*
        Probability of default
    variable, 55
Diversification. *See* Business
Dual rating scales, 60–61
    advantages, 61

Dual-reporting structure,
        advantage, 42

E

EAD. *See* Exposure at default
Earnings volatility, reduction, 53
Economic benefits. *See* Banks
Economic capital, 133, 136–138.
        See also Unexpected loss
  accounting measure, 138
  allocations, 141
  decision-making tool, 138–142
  development, 128
  manager, 30
  measurement, 36
  model, benefit, 140–141
  regulatory capital, contrast,
        137–138
  success, formula, 133–134
  usage, 137
Economic incentives, 8–9. *See
        also* Banking
  discovery, 19
  existence. *See* Tangible
        economic incentives;
        Valuable economic
        incentives
EL. *See* Expected loss
Enron, aberrations, 117
Enterprise risk management
        (ERM)
  bank culture, relationship, 25
  benefits, 34
  business case, 1, 7–9
  business strategy, 3, 5
    proof, 18
  challenge, 29
  committee
    charter, 177–178
    responsibilities, 50
  contrast. *See* Risk silos
  definition, expansion, 4
  development, 44
  driver, identification, 5–6
  evolution, 5–6
  executives
    knowledge, value, 21
    responsibility, 19
  functionality, 29–31
  guidelines, usage, 31
  impact. *See* U.S. banking
        industry
  initiative, reports, 18
  integration, 123–124
  internal audit, role, 40–44
  maximization, 27
    infrastructure, 51–52
  overhead, level, 20
  organizational chart, 179
  plan, transplantation, 23
  practicalities, 44
  practices
    adoption, 1
    initiation, costs, 11
  process
    application, 34
    bank board delegation, 48–49
  regulatory exercise,
        perception, 18
  relationship. *See* Banks;
        Financial management
  standard, 127
  strategic decision, 3, 11
  structure, 31–34
    integration, advantages, 32
  success, formula, 3, 28
  tools, purpose, 107
  traditional definition, 4–5
  understanding, 4–7
  value-added proposition, 20
Enterprise risk management
        (ERM) bank executive
  appointment, 20
  opportunity, 22

Enterprise risk management (ERM) bank executive—*(Cont.)*
  success, 23
  usurper, perception, 19–20
Enterprise risk management (ERM) function
  audit functions, separation, 41
  establishment, 33
  impediments, 33
  importance, 39
  success, 23
Enterprise risk management (ERM) program
  development, 31
  effectiveness, 33
  integration, 33
Enterprise risk manager, responsibility, 19
Enterprise-wide capital measures, 136
Enterprise-wide risk information, 21
Equity-to-assets ratio, 135
Erisk, 138
Event risk, measurement, 130
Executive management buy-in. *See* Corporate-wide initiative
Executive stock sales, SEC inquiries, 95
Expected loss (EL), 61–67, 139
  bank tolerance, 62–63
  components, tolerance levels (understanding), 66
  equation, 130
  explanation, 87
  insights, 62–64
  level, 65
  management expectations, 66–67
  matrix, usage, 66
  risks, acceptance, 64–66
  variable, 55
Expected operational loss, 87
Exposure at default (EAD), 57, 60
  Basel II definition, 60
  tolerance, incorporation, 66
Exposure levels, introduction, 66

F

Fair and Accurate Credit Transactions (FACT) Act, 99
FDIC. *See* Federal Deposit Insurance Corporation
FDICIA. *See* Federal Deposit Insurance Corporation Improvement Act
Federal banking regulators, 40
Federal Deposit Insurance Corporation (FDIC), 7
  Compliance Handbook, 104
  regulator, interagency policy statement, 40
Federal Deposit Insurance Corporation Improvement Act (FDICIA), 18
Federal Express (FedEx), culture (example), 13
Federal Reserve, 7
  2005 Bank Holding Company Rating System, 5
  independence, importance (confirmation), 38–39
  regulator, interagency policy statement, 40
Federal Reserve Bank
  2005 rating system, 9
  LGD adoption, 55
Federal Reserve Bank of Kansas City, 2002 white paper, 99
Federal Reserve Board of New York, 6–7

Index

Financial intermediaries, 71
Financial losses, 71
Financial management, ERM (relationship), 29
Financial reporting, 36
  accuracy, 42
  risks, 43
Fitch (rating agency), 58
Full-time CRO, hiring/assigning, 44–48

G

Gambling, increase, 15
Gap analysis, 129
Gramm-Leach-Bliley Act (GLBA), 18

H

High-quality loans, representation, 62
Historical data, basis, 61
Home Mortgage Disclosure Act (HMDA), 99
  data, 101
Hurdle rates, 139–140
  change, 141

I

IIA. *See* Institute of Internal Auditors
Income, increase, 4
Independence testing, frequency/scope, 105
Infrastructure
  creation, 27
  support, 19
Inherent risk, perception, 87–88
Institute of Internal Auditors (IIA), 41
Insurance companies (market value), risk events (impact), 117

Insurance underwriters, perspective, 10
Interest rates
  changes, 71, 129
  forecast, 72
Interest-rate risk, 72
  exposure, 33
  measurement, 129
  level, management, 72
  reduction tool, 21
Internal audit
  consideration, 41
  coordination, 31
  function, 41
  independence, 43
  relegation, 42
  integration. *See* Risk management
  role, 28. *See also* Enterprise risk management
  elevation, 18
  loss, 42
Internal auditing roles, 41
Internal controls
  assessment, 43
  structure, assessment, 38
  system, 91
  weak system, 49
Internal rating scale. *See* Banks
Internal ratings-based measure, availability, 7
Internal regulatory risk assessments, importance, 102
Internal risk-rating system, usage, 63
Internal/external fraud, 139
Internal/external oversight, absence, 111
International Center for Business Information, Risk Management 2004 Conference, 38

222 *Index*

Investments
  risk, 75
  secondary marketability, 73
  VAR, 77

J

Job descriptions, 147–162
Johnson & Johnson, Tylenol impact, 96

L

LBOs. *See* Leveraged buyouts
Legal compliance departments, usage, 40
Legal risk, 89–92
  evaluation, 111–112
  identification/measurement, 90–91
  level, categorization, 91
  mitigation, 91–92
  summary, 92
Lending
  decisions, 64
  opportunities, 64
Leverage ratio, 135
Leveraged buyouts (LBOs), PD level, 63–64
LGD. *See* Loss given default
LGE. *See* Loss given the event
Liability modeling, supplantation, 35
LIED. *See* Loss in the Event of Default
Lien position, 60
Liquidity
  determination, 73
  risk, 73
Loans
  characteristics, bank executive examination, 67
  commitments. *See* Unfunded loan commitments

defaults, occurrence (estimation), 35
facility
  potential loss, severity, 55
  types, 60
loss provision, 131
portfolio
  criteria, 66
  risk levels, measurement, 7
quantity, usage, 63
review division, 31
review function, reliance, 34–35
securing. *See* Working capital loan
Loss. *See* Expected loss
  magnitude, 87
  probability, example. *See* Probability of loss
  provisions, 78
  risk, 86
Loss given default (LGD), 59–60
  adoption. *See* Federal Reserve Bank
  combination. *See* Probability of default
  limitation, 64
  range, 61
  representation, 65
  usage, 55
Loss given the event (LGE), 130
Loss in the Event of Default (LIED), 55

M

Macroeconomic environment, 59
Market risk, 69, 81
  assessment, 40
  division, 31
  measurement, 128–129
    methodology, 126
  success, formula, 69–70
  types, 71

Marsh & McLennan (market value, decrease), 117
Mature risk, 71–73
  perspective, 70
McDonough, William J., 6
McKinsey & Company, client work, 8
Measurement. *See* Risk
  impact. *See* Capabilities
  problem, 15
Measures, addition, 18
Media, negative coverage, 109
  tracking, 114
Middle market companies, credit ratings (absence), 58
Money laundering reporting, 111
Moody's Investor Service, 58
  perspective, 10
  rating, 59
Morgan Stanley, sex discrimination lawsuit, 94
Mortgage loan, exposure, 33
Murphy's Law, 83

N

NASDAQ regulations, 35
Net interest income (NII), change, 129
New Basel Capital Accord
  design, 7
  drafting, 6
NII. *See* Net interest income
Non-Basel II banks,
  problems, 9
Noninsured investment,
  consideration, 75

O

Office of the Comptroller of the Currency (OCC), 7
  regulator, interagency policy statement, 40

Office of Thrift Supervision (OTS), 7
  regulator, interagency policy statement, 40
Operating budget, approval, 39
Operating expenses, decrease, 8
Operational loss. *See* Expected operational loss; Unexpected operational loss
  identification/loss/ evaluation, 84
  reduction, 8
Operational risk, 83, 121
  assessment, 35
    process, 109–110
  Basel II focus, 85
  categories, review, 111
  definition, 86
  division, 31
  evaluation
    process, 110–111
    tools, 107–119
    tools, usage, 111–119
  existence, 83
  identification process, 108–109
    improvement, 9
  management
    fundamentals, 85–88
    iterative process, 107–111
  measurement, 130
    improvement, 9
    methodology, 126
    provisions, 6
  relegation, 35
  sub-components, 107
  success, formula, 83–84
  types, 88–107
Organization
  economic incentives. *See* Banking
  risk tolerance, 16
  threats, 19

Organization-wide profitability, 21
OTS. *See* Office of Thrift Supervision
Out-of-pocket losses, 71
Overhead
  level. *See* Enterprise risk management
  unnecessity, 25

P

Paid-in capital, 137
Patriot Act, 99
PD. *See* Probability of default
Performance
  evaluation, preparation, 39
  measurement, problem, 136
  reviews, 38
Pigs in the parlor, analogy, 16, 18
PNC Financial Services, 43
Portfolio
  decisions, 64
  managers, 64
    matrix, usage, 66
  risk levels, measurement. *See* Loans
  theory, 129
Pretax earnings, improvement, 8
Pricing decisions, improvement, 8
Privacy rules, 111
Probabilities, calculation. *See* Banks
Probability of default (PD), 57–59
  level. *See* Leveraged buyouts
  LGD, combination, 63, 64
  range, 61
  ratings, 59
Probability of loss, example, 79
Products, risk profile, 9
Profitability, response, 53
Publicly held company, financial market evaluation, 93

Q

Quantitative analysts (quants), 135
  hiring, 31

R

RAROC. *See* Risk-adjusted return of capital
Rating agencies, risk management perspective, 10–11
Rating transition experience, tracking, 58
Regulatory capital
  contrast. *See* Economic capital
  defining, 137
Regulatory compliance, ensuring, 106
Regulatory guidance, 48
Regulatory risk, 89, 97–106
  assessments. *See* Internal regulatory risk assessments
  compliance function, defining, 98–100
  convenience, 35
  culture/structure, 101
  division, 31
  function, management, 103
  governance, 101–102
  independence, 104–105
  management, 106
  mitigation, 100
  program, absence, 98
  summary, 105–106
Reputation risk, 89, 93–97
  assessment process, 114–117
  definition, 96
  evaluation, 112–118
    process, 117–118
  events, casualties, 94
  identification process, 112–114
  impact. *See* Business

management, 95–96
summary, 97
Return, probability, 75
Return on equity (ROE), 140
Riggs (bank), regulation violations, 17
Risk. *See* Interest-rate risk; Liquidity risk; Market risk; Mature risk; Strategic risk
  acceptance, 110
  alignment, 34, 36
  analysis, 46
  analytics, addition, 22
  appetite, 29–30. *See also* Banks
  assessment, 16, 30
    enhancement, 34
    outsourcing, 32
  assessors, experience, 46
  awareness. *See* Bank culture
    construction, strategies, 16–19
  benchmarks, 30
  business ownership, 34
  consideration, 22. *See also* Strategic decision making
  control, absence, 88
  coordinator, appointment, 36
  culture/structure. *See* Regulatory risk
  effects, focus, 34
  elements, incorporation, 36
  elimination, 37, 90
  evaluation. *See* Legal risk; Reputation risk
  tools. *See* Operational risk events
    impact. *See* Banks; Insurance companies
  events, prediction. *See* Catastrophic risk events
  factors, enterprise-wide appraisals, 53
  functions. *See* Bank risk
  governance. *See* Regulatory risk
  grades, 66
  identification, 30. *See also* Legal risk
    enhancement, 34
    sources, 113
  internal controls, identification, 85–86
  level, value (assignation), 37
  limits, 91
  matrix, plotting, 115
  measurement, 127–128. *See also* Banking; Credit risk; Event risk; Legal risk; Operational risk
    dimensions, establishment, 62
    methodology, 10
  measures, complexity range, 132
  mismanagement, price, 4
  mitigation, 110. *See also* Legal risk
  monitoring
    functions, 40
    practices, 91
  perception. *See* Inherent risk
  portfolio, management, 85
  prioritization, 36
  profiles, 22, 23, 181–188
  quantification, 109–110
  reallocation, 92
  reduction, 21
    benefits, 22
  reports, 37, 181–188
  retention, 110
  reward
    contrast, sensitivity, 40
    trade-off, 118

Risk—(Cont.)
  takers, employees
    (exclusion), 38
  taking, 37
  term, etymology, 3
  tolerance. See Organization
  trends, 37
  types, 69. See also Operational
    risk
  unexpected loss. See Value-at-
    risk
  variables, response, 53
  visibility, elevation (CRO
    impact), 48
Risk management, 73. See also
    Corporate level;
    Reputation risk
  approaches, 19
  board of directors,
    perception, 5
  conduit, 47
  consultants, 45
    risk management
      opportunity, 47
  costs, 135
  division, existence, 31
  efforts
    management usage, 34
    undertaking, 36
  fad, perception, 27
  forms, 37
  function, 42
    CEO skepticism, 24
    role, 34–36
  internal audit, integration, 44
  issues, 36
  management role,
    delegation, 48
  meaning, 3
  methodologies,
    establishment, 41
  objectives, board of director
    definitions, 30–31
  organizational structure, exis-
    tence, 28
  plan, 163–164
  policy, 165–172
  prior experience, 44–45
  procedures, 173–176
  processes, evolution, 43
  program, 90, 91
    tailoring, 30
  promotion, 28
  reports, 49–50
  strategic business
    decision, 31
  structures, development, 29
  Taoism, antithesis, 27
Risk Management Association, 135
Risk managers, 45
  compensation/promotion, 38
  development, 31
  reporting lines,
    independence, 38
  risk management
    opportunity, 46
Risk profile report, sample,
  181–188
Risk silos
  ERM, contrast, 32–33
  tolerance, 32
  usage, 51
Risk-adjusted performance
  measures, 136
Risk-adjusted profitability
  measurement, 131
Risk-adjusted return of capital
  (RAROC), 123, 136
  measurement, 36
  number, 139
  usage, 134, 140–141
    importance, 137

Index

Risk-averse culture strategies, 17–18
Risk-aware culture, 15
  creation, 31
Risk-based capital, calculation, 78–79
Risk-based decisions, 22
  making, 34
Risk-based measure, 141
Risk-based pricing, 131
Risk-based top-down supervisory approach, 102
Risk-conscious culture, establishment, 36
Risk-neutral company, 18
Risk-neutral culture strategies, 18
Risk-reporting structures, development, 29
Risk-tolerant culture strategies, 18–19
ROE. *See* Return on equity

S

Sarbanes-Oxley (SOX)
  Act, 4, 24
    impact, 92
    Section 404, 43
    compliance, 4
  ERM, connection, 18
SARs filings, 17
Scenario analysis, 118–119
Securities and Exchange Commission (SEC)
  inquiries. *See* Executive stock sales
  regulations, 35
Self-assessments, requirement, 113
Senior executives
  ERM responsibility, 29
  participation, 36
Senior managers, reports (preparation), 36
Services, risk profile, 9
Shareholder equity, book value, 137
Shareholder value
  addition, 47
  manager, 30
Shareholder value-added (SVA), 139, 141–142
  equation, 141
Single-dimension scales, 60
Single-dimension system, 61
SOX. *See* Sarbanes-Oxley
Spitzer, Eliot (actions), 117
Stakeholders
  advocacy groups, 109
  collaboration, 45
  communication, 31
  persuasion, 45
  reports, preparation, 36
Standard & Poor's (S&P), 58
  perspective, 10
  rating, 59
  tool, 67
Standard deviation, equation, 130
State consumer protection statutes, 111
State licensing rules, 111
Stock values, response, 117
Strategic business decision. *See* Risk management
Strategic decision. *See* Enterprise risk management
Strategic decision making, risk (consideration), 31
Strategic planning
  improvement, 131
  processes, 137

Strategic risk, 89, 106–107
  management plan, 30
Supervision, top down
  approach, 101

T

Tangible economic incentives,
  existence, 4
Tao of Risk Management, 27
Taoism, antithesis. *See* Risk management
Threats, 17. *See also* Organization management, 20
  removal/neutralization, 18
Tier-1 capital, 137
Transaction process errors,
  risk, 86

U

Unenforceable contracts, 90
Unexpected loss (UL), 139. *See also* Value-at-risk
  concept, 78
  economic capital, 78
  equation, 130–131
Unexpected operational loss, 87
Unfunded loan commitments, 60
U.S. Armed Forces,
  shortages, 125
U.S. banking industry, ERM
  impact, 9–11
U.S. federal banking agencies,
  determination. *See*
  Advanced-risk
  methodology
U.S. Postal Service (U.S.P.S.),
  culture (example), 13

U.S. Sentencing Guidelines
  amendments, 24
  revisions, 92

V

Valuable economic incentives,
  existence, 4
Value creation, 136–137
Value-added. *See* Shareholder
  value-added
  proposition, 20. *See also*
  Enterprise risk
  management
Value-at-risk (VAR), 73–80, 123
  approach, 87
  calculation, 75
  communication, 77–78
  limitations, 130
  measurement, 36, 72
  measures, usage, 70
  methodology, 73
  models, 4
  translation, 77
  unexpected loss, 78–80
  usage, 81

W

Wall Street
  perspective, 10
  risk management perspective,
  10
Washington Mutual Inc., 43
What if evaluation, 91
Working capital loan,
  securing, 61
Worst-case evaluation, 91